DISEMBODIED LAUGHTER
TROILUS AND THE APOTHEOSIS TRADITION

DISEMBODIED LAUGHTER
TROILUS AND
THE APOTHEOSIS TRADITION

A Reexamination of Narrative
and Thematic Contexts

John M. Steadman

UNIVERSITY OF CALIFORNIA PRESS

Berkeley Los Angeles London 1972

University of California Press
Berkeley and Los Angeles, California
University of California Press, Ltd.
London, England

Copyright © 1972 by The Regents of the University of California
ISBN: 0-520-02047-2
Library of Congress Catalog Card Number: 71-634791
Printed in the United States of America

Ad patrem

. . . nec novimus ipsi
Aptiùs à nobis quae possint munera donis
Respondere tuis, quamvis nec maxima possint
Respondere tuis, nedum ut par gratia donis
Esse queat, vacuis quae redditur arida verbis.

PREFACE

The sound of words, Chaucer informs us, is "noght but eyr ybroken," and Fame herself has pitched her mansion in the upper atmosphere. Poetic reputations, like the glory of kings and warriors, are subject to meteorological disturbances, to changing climates of opinion, and the variable pressures of rising critical standards or declining tastes. Not unsurprisingly, both *Troilus and Criseyde* and *Paradise Lost* have frequently been in the epicenter of such storms—gusty yet fruitful disputes that have uprooted established dogmas but nurtured a promising undergrowth of green and burgeoning theories in their stead.

To some of us, the critical tempests over Chaucer's epilogue and Milton's Satan may seem very much alike. Both poets have been accused not only of inconsistency but, in a sense, of aesthetic hypocrisy. Both, it is charged, contradict themselves, first creating a vivid and convincing portrait and afterward refuting it through moral comments or narrative additions incompatible with what has gone before. In both instances the poet arbitrarily employs a "technique of degradation." Just as Milton destroys his superb archangel (who, like the djinn released from the bottle, has swollen to heroic dimensions and seems altogether too dangerous to leave uncorked), Chaucer retracts his encomium of chivalric love and courtly adultery. In both cases, it is alleged, the poet's ethical commentary contradicts the evidence of plot and character; his moral "allegations" clash with his narrative "demonstrations." In both cases his refutation is extraneous to the poetic fable. Whatever its ethical force, it is aesthetically invalid. Artistically, it is no true refutation at all, merely a sophistical elench.

Professor Curry has condemned Chaucer's epilogue as "a nest of contradictions"; in his opinion, it is both artistically and thematically irrelevant. Other critics acknowledge its compatibility with ideas expressed earlier in the poem, but sometimes deplore the conventions that induced the poet to graft an otherworldly morality upon a sophisticated and worldly romance. To another observer, the epilogue seems the logical culmination of the hero's fidelity to the principles of courtly love; Troilus receives the high reward his constancy has merited. In the opinion of other scholars, the epilogue constitutes a decisive rejection of the ideals and conventions of courtly love. Finally, others would regard "courtly love" itself as an anachronism and perhaps a myth. The primary tensions within the poem spring (it would appear) less from the opposition between *curteisye* and *vileinye* than from the antithesis between earthly and heavenly love.

These are high matters, and like Donne one might wish that "some old lover's ghost"—possibly Troilus, or even Chaucer himself—might be conjured up to resolve them. But perhaps, like Palamon and the good Parson, he would merely advise one to leave the answer to divines or to the "correccioun of clerkes."

The following essay is essentially a study of narrative and thematic contexts, reexamining Chaucer's flight episode against the background of the apotheosis tradition and the conventions of classical pneumatology and exploring its thematic relationships with the poem as a whole and the epilogue in particular. The first and second chapters are concerned with the question of the "eighth sphere" and classical conceptions of Elysium. The third reinvestigates similarities and differences between Chaucer's flight sequence and its major analogues in Lucan and Cicero, Dante and Boccaccio. The fourth chapter, in turn, reexamines its relationship to the Boethian insertions in Books III and IV of the *Troilus* and the dream episode in Book V. The fifth chapter explores its position in the Boethian framework of the poem, while the sixth and seventh chapters reconsider its immediate context in the epilogue. In exploring this tradition, I have quoted at length from medieval and Renaissance commentaries on Lucan's *Pharsalia* and Boethius's *De consolatione philosophiae*. These are interesting for the light they throw on the continuity and divergences between medieval and Renaissance tradition.

At the outset, I should like to emphasize the limited scope of this study. In an age of lunar landings and interplanetary rockets, it is refreshing to contemplate the astronautical feats of our ancestors: their space probes conducted with so little strain on the national budget and so little cost to the imagination; their interstellar voyages accomplished without benefit of nuclear fuels and electronic controls, but through the inexhaustible resources of Neoplatonic metaphysics and Stoic eschatology. Nevertheless, there were so many of these astral pioneers, that to give them their due—to bestow even superficial justice—would take us far beyond the scope of this study. Plato's Er was one such voyager, Ovid's Caesar another. To these we must add Saint Paul and Mohammed and Gautama. Some were visionaries, prophets, or poets. Some were philosophers or satirists. Some were Gnostic heretics; some were canonized saints. Some were shamans. Some were the *manes* of governors and warriors; some were mythical *ingénus* like Icarus and Phaehton. Some were heroes of chivalric romance like Astolfo. Some were the protagonists of science fiction. Some made their ascent by eagle or fiery chariot or hippogriff, some by geese and moonshine, some by dialectical plumage. Some relied on the natural levity of flame to carry them back to the fiery regions from which they had come; others depended on the viewless wings of poesy or the feathers of imagination. Some journeyed in order to learn the state of souls after death, some to enjoy the reward of meritorious deeds, some to reach the habitation of Fame, some to recover sanity. Some took their seats in the firmament among the fixed stars, some among the planets. Some ascended to the Empyrean itself; others soared no higher than the lunar vault or the upper reaches of the air.[1]

[1] Aspects of the astral flight tradition have been discussed by Franz Cumont, *Astrology and Religion among the Greeks and Romans* (New York and London, 1912); Cumont, *After Life in Roman Paganism* (New Haven, 1922); Cumont, "Le mysticisme astral dans l'antiquité," *Bulletin*, Académie Royale de Belgique, 4th ser. (1909), pp. 258 ff., 278ff.; Martin P. Nilsson, *Greek Piety*, trans. Herbert Jennings Rose (New York, 1969), pp. 101-102, 125, 129, 135, 146, 163; Morton W. Bloomfield, *The Seven Deadly Sins, An Introduction to the History of A Concept, with Special Reference to Medieval*

The force that thrust them to such giddy heights (and sometimes kept them there) was, in the final analysis, the power of
tradition. They achieved their exaltation through the beliefs and
phantasies, the intellectual and poetic conventions, of the societies
that heroized or satirized them; perhaps they can be adequately
interpreted only within the context of these cultures. The

English Literature (Lansing, Mich., 1952), pp. 12-26, 313-326, and *passim*.
Professor Bloomfield's useful bibliography calls attention to the studies
by Wilhelm Bousset, "Die Himmelreise der Seele," *Archiv für Religions-
wissenschaft*, IV (1901), 136ff., 229 ff.; by Carl Hoenn, *Studien zur Geschichte
der Himmelfahrt im klassischen Altertum* (Mannheim, 1910); by Louis
Rougier, *L'Origine astronomique de la croyance pythagoracienne en l'immor-
talité céleste des âmes* (Cairo, 1933); and by C. Fritzsche, *Die lateinischen
Visionen des Mittelalters bis zur Mitte des* 12.*Jahrhunderts*, *Romanische
Forschungen*, vol. II (1886), III (1887). For the history of this motif in
Gnosticism, see Hans Jonas, *The Gnostic Religion*, 2d ed. rev. (Boston, 1963);
and for Hermetic examples, see Frances A. Yates, *Giordano Bruno and the
Hermetic Tradition* (New York, 1969), pp. 24-25, 137, 236-239, 249-250. For
the vision of the other world in Islamic and Judaeo-Christian tradition, see
Miguel Asín Palacios, *La eschatologia musulmana en la Divina Comedia*
(Madrid, 1919); Asín Palacios, *Islam and the Divine Comedy*, trans. and abr.
Harold Sunderland (New York, 1926); R. H. Charles, *Apocrypha and
Pseudepigrapha of the Old Testament* (Oxford, 1913); James Hastings, ed.,
Encyclopaedia of Religion and Ethics (New York and London, 1926), *s.v.*
"Blest, Abode of the" and "Eschatology"; *The Jewish Encyclopedia* (New York
and London, 1901), *s.v.* "Apocalyptic Literature." For shamanistic elements in
the journey to the heavens or the underworld, see Nora K. Chadwick and
Victor Zhirmunsky, *Oral Epics of Central Asia* (Cambridge, 1969), pp. 119,
123-136, 234-267; Nora K. Chadwick, "The Spiritual Ideas and Experiences of
the Tatars of Central Asia," *Journal of the Royal Anthropological Institute*,
LXVI (1936), 291 ff.; C. M. Bowra, *Heroic Poetry* (London, 1964), pp. 6-7,
18-20. For analogues in world literature see Stith Thompson, *Motif-Index of
Folk-Literature* (Helsinki, 1932-1936), D2135, FO-199, V511 ("Magic air
journey," "Other world journeys," "Visions of the other world"). For aspects
of the scientific or pseudoscientific flight to the heavens, see Marjorie Hope
Nicolson, *Voyages to the Moon* (New York, 1948); Gunnar Qvarnström, *Dikten
och den Nya Vetenskapen. Det Astronautiska Motivet*, Societatis Humaniorum
Litterarum Lundensis, no. XL (Lund, 1961). For the tradition of "réflexion sur
l'étroitesse de la terre, considérée d'en haut," see Pierre Courcelle, *La
Consolation de Philosophie dans la Tradition Littéraire, Antécédents et Postérité
de Boèce* (Paris, 1967), pp. 355-372, appendix II, "La vision cosmique de
Boèce et de saint Benoît."

traditions themselves, though frequently interrelated, are too complex and too diverse to fall within a single field of study. They require the specialized techniques of a variety of disciplines, and the literary historian must be content to surrender certain territory without contest to his rivals—to the anthropologist, the theologian, the historian of science, and the student of intellectual history. Even after drastic partition the field that remains is too large for one man to plow, and I shall be content with something less than Piers's half acre.[2]

For similar reasons I have resisted the temptation to discuss the ascent motif in Chaucer's *House of Fame*.[3] As this concerns another (though related) facet of the flight tradition, it presents rather different problems and merits a separate study.

With minor changes the first chapter formed the nucleus of a paper I read at the University of California, Los Angeles, on April 9, 1970. I am grateful to Professors Florence Ridley and Robert Kinsman for inviting me to participate in the program, and to Professor William Matthews for moderating the discus-

[2] One additional point requires clarification. In examining the tradition of Pompey's "apotheosis" in medieval and early Renaissance commentaries and in discussing the impact of the apotheosis tradition on Boccaccio and Chaucer, I shall employ this term in its broader rather than its more literal sense. Lucan appears to have "heroized" Pompey rather than deified him. Though Roman emperors might achieve posthumous divinity and Neoplatonic sages become reunited (and indeed identified) with the supreme deity, there is, of course, no actual deification in the case of Troilus and Arcita. Though several commentators refer to Pompey's ascent as an apotheosis or deification, these terms are not, as a rule, to be taken literally. Near the end of Book VIII, in contrasting the Senate's official deification of Julius Caesar with its failure to restore Pompey's remains to Italian soil, Lucan argues that Pompey deserves divine honors, associates him with the goddess Fortune as highest deity ("Nunc est pro numine summo Hoc tumulo Fortuna iacens"), and foresees a time when his cult may rival that of Jove. Near the end of book VI, the ghost of a dead soldier prophesies to Pompey's son that a place in the brighter portion of the infernal kingdom ("regnique in parte serena") has been set aside for the shades of Pompey and his family.

[3] Cf. also the motif of contemplation of the Galaxy and the vision of "al the world" as "No more . . . than a prikke" in *The House of Fame*, lines 904 ff.

sion. It is a pleasure to express my gratitude to Professor Bernard F. Huppé for his stimulating course on Chaucer during my postgraduate training, to the Chaucerian studies of other scholars at Princeton—Professors Gordon Hall Gerould, D. W. Robertson, Jr., and R. K. Root—and to my colleagues at the Henry E. Huntington Library and the University of California, Riverside.

John M. Steadman

The Henry E. Huntington Library
San Marino, California

CONTENTS

CHAPTER I

THE EIGHTH SPHERE
LUNAR CONCAVE OR STELLAR VAULT?

In antiquity departed warriors did not fade away. They were decently cremated or quietly stellified. The less adventurous and the more worldly clung to their *heroa*—barrows, mausolea, and cairns. The more enterprising set forth on subterranean or supra-terrestrial journeys, anticipating the science fiction of H. G. Wells and Jules Verne. Several became gods and acquired the privileges of Olympus. More than a few—Aeneas, Anchises, Pompey, and perhaps Arcita and Troilus—attained Elysium. This, like Utopia, might be nowhere—or almost anywhere, provided it was sufficiently remote. Reliable authority placed it beyond the western ocean or in the Antipodes, under the earth, in the upper regions of the air or in the lunar concave.

1

Chaucer tells us little about Troilus's final destination. Following Boccaccio's account of Arcita, he merely informs us that his hero went where Mercury—Hermes Psychopompos, guide of souls—"sorted him to dwell." On the immediate end of these journeys, however, both poets are quite specific. Arcita soars toward the "concave of the eighth heaven"—"ver la concavità del cielo ottava." Troilus similarly ascends to the concave of the seventh or eighth sphere.

The problem of identifying this region depends primarily on two factors, both highly debatable. First, did Chaucer write "seventh" or "eighth"? The majority of manuscripts contain the former reading, but the latter version is closer to Chaucer's immediate source for the flight episode, Boccaccio's *Teseida*. Second, did Chaucer number his spheres outward from the moon, or inward from the sphere of the fixed stars? Or, in fact, did he begin with the outermost sphere of all—the primum mobile? On both these questions, answers have varied widely. Professors Cope and Scott believe that Chaucer deliberately altered Boccaccio's "ottava" to "seventh," but they nevertheless number the planets differently. Whereas Cope places Troilus on Saturn, Scott assigns him to the planet Mercury.[1]

Other scholars prefer the reading "eighth," but thereafter disagree as to the order in which the planets should be numbered. For Root and Robinson, Chaucer's eighth sphere was probably the moon. Both Dobson and Bloomfield, however, maintain that Chaucer must have placed his hero in the sphere of the fixed stars—the *aplanes* or firmament.[2]

---

[1] Jackson I. Cope, "Chaucer, Venus and the 'Seventhe Spere,'" *MLN*, LXVII (1952), 245-246; Forrest S. Scott, "The Seventh Sphere: A Note on *Troilus and Criseyde*," *MLR*, LI (1956), 2-5; John W. Clark, "Dante and the Epilogue of the *Troilus*," *JEGP*, L (1951), 1-10, argues that Boccaccio clearly "conceived Arcita's spirit as in the lunar sphere" but that Chaucer "chose to leave Troilus' precise station undefined."

[2] Morton W. Bloomfield, "The Eighth Sphere: A Note on Chaucer's *Troilus and Criseyde*, V, 1809," *MLR*, LIII (1958), 408-410; E. J. Dobson, "Some Notes on Middle English Texts," *English and Germanic Studies*, Unviersity of Birmingham, I (1947-1948), 61-62; Robert Kilburn Root, ed., *The Book of Troilus and Criseyde* (Princeton, 1926), pp. 560-562; F. N. Robinson, ed., *The Works of Geoffrey Chaucer*, 2d. ed. (Boston, 1957), p. 837. See also Bloomfield, "Distance and Predestination in *Troilus and Criseyde*," *PMLA*, LXXII (1957), 14-26; Bloomfield, *The Seven Deadly Sins*, pp. 16-17 ff. For a review of recent scholarship of "the question of Troilus' exact position at the end of the poem," see Chauncey Wood, "Chaucer and Astrology," in *Companion to Chaucer Studies*, ed. Beryl Rowland (Toronto, 1968), p. 196. Peter Dronke, "The Conclusion of Troilus and Criseyde," *Medium AEvum*, XXXIII (1964), 47-52, argues that Chaucer's eighth sphere must be that of the fixed stars, inasmuch as he had already alluded to Venus, in the prologue to Book III of the *Troilus*, as the "thridde heven." In a more recent study, Professor Wood argues that "Bloomfield's adduction of the eighth sphere of the fixed stars as a traditional place for dead pagans offers us a way of understanding where both Boccaccio's Arcita and Chaucer's Troilus were positioned, providing we are willing to grant them at least some degree of gnosis." Citing Boethius' allusions to the ascent of the soul and Chaucer's references to 'likerous folk' in the *Parliament of Fowls*, Wood suggests that

These problems are further complicated by the question of Boccaccio's direct and Chaucer's indirect sources. Both Root and Tatlock stress the influence of Cicero's *Somnium Scipionis*. Scott emphasizes the parallel with Lucan's *Pharsalia*. Dobson argues the influence of Dante's *Paradiso*. Patch and Owen maintain that Chaucer's epilogue reflects the influence of Boethius. Bloomfield points to the widespread belief that the souls of departed worthies ascended to the firmament—the "ogdoad". Accordingly, he approves Dobson's view that Troilus ascended to the sphere of the fixed stars.[3]

"in remanding Troilus to the eighth sphere of the fixed stars, Chaucer sends him as one who is 'likerous' to a place where the wise pause for some time and the lecherous must remain 'Tyl many a world be passed.'" See Wood, "Troilus among the Spheres: A Survey and a Suggestion," in *Chaucer and the Country of the Stars: Poetic Uses of Astrological Imagery* (Princeton, 1970), pp. 180-191.

[3] John S. P. Tatlock, "The Epilog of Chaucer's *Troilus*," *MP*, XVIII (1920-1921), 625-659; Howard R. Patch, "Troilus on Determinism," *Speculum*, VI (1929), 225-243; Charles A. Owen, Jr., "The Significance of Chaucer's Revisions of *Troilus and Criseyde*," *MP*, LV (1957-1958), 1-5; Theodore A. Stroud, "Boethius' Influence on Chaucer's *Troilus*," *MP*, XLIX (1951-1952), 1-9. Clark ("Dante and the Epilogue") suggests that Chaucer's mind was "full of the *Divine Comedy*, and probably also of the *Somnium Scipionis*. . . ." Walter Clyde Curry, *Chaucer and the Mediaeval Sciences*, rev. and enl. (New York, 1960), pp. 347-348, argues that Boccaccio's flight stanzas were dependent on Cicero's *Somnium Scipionis*, but cites additional parallels in Clement and Origen. Alfred L. Kellogg, "On the Tradition of Troilus's Vision of the Little Earth," *Mediaeval Studies*, XXII (1960), 204-213, suggests that "the Christian language of Boccaccio's passage is attributable less to Dante than to Boccaccio's use of a previously unnoticed source"—a "commentary on Isaiah XL as incorporated into the *Somme le Roi* of Frère Lorens." The influence of Lucan has been suggested by Thomas Tyrwhitt, *The Poetical Works of Geoffrey Chaucer* (London, 1843), p. lvi; by Scott, "Seventh Sphere"; and by Patch, "Chauceriana," *Englische Studien*, LXV (1930-1931), 357-359. In "Fate in Boethius and the Neoplatonists," *Speculum*, IV (1929), 68-69n., Patch cites Cicero, Lucan, and Prudentius as parallels. The studies by Tatlock, Owen, Stroud, and others have been collected in *Chaucer Criticism*, vol. II, *Troilus and Criseyde and the Minor Poems*, ed. Richard J. Schoeck and Jerome Taylor (Notre Dame, 1961).

With the multiplication of analogues, critics have felt com-pelled to distinguish between major and minor sources. In ident-ifying Boccaccio's "cielo ottava" with the sphere of the fixed stars, Dobson based his argument largely on the influence of Dante's *Commedia*. Boccaccio's principal source (he suggested) was not the *Somnium Scipionis* or the *Pharsalia*, but the twenty-second canto of the *Paradiso*. From the sphere of the fixed stars Dante looks down on the planetary orbs and smiles at the "vile sem-blance" of the earth, so insignificant in comparison with the heavens.

Boccaccio's sources may throw light on his own meaning, but they are relevant to the *Troilus* only insofar as Chaucer himself was aware of them. He certainly knew the *Somnium Scipionis* and the *Commedia*, and probably the *Pharsalia*. A few stanzas after the flight passage, he quotes other lines from the *Paradiso*; and shortly before the flight stanzas, he pays homage to Lucan, among other poets. Moreover, Professor Shannon has noted other instances of apparent indebtedness to the *Pharsalia* elsewhere in Chaucer's poetry.

If Chaucer was indeed conscious of these three analogues when he translated Boccaccio's flight passage, they would not only have strengthened the latter's authority with that of more illustrious writers—Cicero, Lucan, and Dante—but they could also have conditioned the use Chaucer himself made of the *Teseida*. In Troilus's flight we may recognize a tradition that embraces Lucan and Cicero, Dante and Boccaccio, and that also displays marked affinities with Boethius's *De Consolatione*. We should not rule out the probability that Chaucer himself may have been fully aware of these affinities, that he recognized the traditional nature of this motif, and that he may have expected his more judicious readers to interpret it against the background established by medieval and classical analogues.

One of the salient features of medieval commentary on these parallels is its tendency to treat them as facets of a single tradition. In his exposition of the *Paradiso*, Pietro Alighieri cites

Lucan's description of the flight of Pompey's soul.[4] Commentaries on Lucan and Boethius mention Macrobius's exposition of *Scipio's Dream*.[5] The emphasis on *contemptus mundi*, the contrast between temporal and eternal values, and the opposition between earthly ignorance and heavenly knowledge recur in all these analogues. Against this background, the attempt to trace the various details of Arcita's flight to particular sources may seem both arbitrary and misleading. Many of these details are commonplaces of a well-established tradition, and both Chaucer and Boccaccio must have recognized them as such. The attempt to isolate sources may, however, be more reliable when applied to verbal resemblances or even to similar patterns of ideas.

The surviving fragments of Cicero's *Republic* do not tell us precisely where Scipio stood in order to contemplate the galaxy, but Macrobius expressly places him in the Milky Way itself.

[4] *Petri Allegherii super Dantis ipsius genitoris Comoediam commentarium*, ed. Vincentio Nannucci (Florentiae, 1847), pp. 691-692, "Dicendo quomodo in dicta octava sphaera respexit deorsum, idest elevatus a scientia theologica omnia ista mundana vilia sibi et pusilla videbantur. Dicendo quod vidit istum globum, idest terrae et aquae corpus, quod dicitur sphaera globata, ita parvulum et despectum respectu coelestium rerum, quod risit, ideat truffatus est de eo, ut anima Pompeij de suo trunco, Lucano dicente:

> . . . *Postquam se lumine vero*
> *Implevit, stellasque vagas miratur, et astra*
> *Fixa polis, vidit quanta sub nocte jaceret*
> *Nostra dies, risitque sui ludibria trunci.*"

We should note the verbal parallel between Pietro Alighieri's *respectu coelestium rerum* and Boccaccio's "A rispetto del ciel" and Chaucer's "To respect of the pleyn felicite That is in hevene above. . . ." The word *respect* occurs neither in Lucan's lines on Pompey's apotheosis nor in Dante's account of his own *contemptus mundi* in the *Paradiso* analogue. Like Chaucer, Pietro emphasizes the terraqueous globe.

[5] *Commentum duplex in Boetium de consolatione philosophie* (Lyons, 1498, HEH # 100389), hereafter cited as *Boethius: Commentum duplex*. This work contains the commentaries of Pseudo-Aquinas and Iodocus Badius Ascensius. For Dante's relation to Lucan, see Ettore Paratore, *Dante e Lucano* (Torino, 1962) and Vincenzo Ussani, *Dante e Lucano* (Firenze, 1917). For Chaucer's knowledge of Lucan, see Edgar R. Shannon, "Chaucer and Lucan's *Pharsalia*," *MP*, XVI (1919), 609-614.

Pompey's spirit apparently soars to the lunar concave, where the souls of heroes dwell after death. Dante regards the universe from the sphere of the fixed stars. The *contemptus mundi* theme characterizes all these analogues, and the laughter motif occurs in all except *Scipio's Dream*.[6] (As the *Somnium Scipionis* has already received close attention from Chaucer scholars, I shall not re-examine it in detail.)

Lucan's account of Pompey's apotheosis occupies the opening lines of the Ninth Book, following the account of the hero's assassination and decapitation, the desecration of his body, and the efforts of a faithful follower (Cordus, Pompey's *quaestor*) to perform the rites of cremation:[7]

> At non in Pharia manes iacuere favilla,
> Nec cinis exiguus tantam conpescuit umbram:
> Prosiluit busto semustaque membra relinquens
> Degeneremque rogum sequitur convexa Tonantis.
> Qua niger astriferis conectitur axibus aer
> Quodque patet terras inter lunaeque meatus,
> Semidei manes habitant, quos ignea virtus
> Innocuos vita patientes aetheris imi
> Fecit, et aeternos animam collegit in orbes:
> Non illuc auro positi nec ture sepulti
> Perveniunt. Illic postquam se lumine vero
> Inplevit, stellasque vagas miratus et astra
> Fixa polis, vidit quanta sub nocte iaceret
> Nostra dies, risitque sui ludibria trunci.

Or (as Thomas May's literal but uninspired translation renders this passage),[8] the ghost of Pompey quits his body and

---

[6] See Macrobius, *Commentary on the Dream of Scipio*, trans. William Harris Stahl, Columbia University Records of Civilization, Sources and Studies, vol. XLVIII (New York, 1952). In *The Parliament of Fowls* Chaucer interprets Scipio's comparison between "the lytel erthe" and "the hevene quantite" as an exhortation to eschew worldly delight for "hevene blisse."

[7] *Lucan*, trans. J. D. Duff, Loeb Classical Library (London and New York, 1928), p. 504.

[8] *Lucan's Pharsalia*, trans. Thomas May (London, 1631, HEH # 62414), pp. 209-210. According to the summary of the argument, "*Pompey's* departed

                    . . . takes
Up to the convexe of the sky his flight,
Where with blacke ayre the starry poles doe meete.
The space betwixt the regions of the moone,
And earth, halfe-deify'd soules possesse alone,
Whom fiery worth, in guiltlesse lives, has taught
To brooke the lower part of heaven, and brought
Them to th' aeternall sphaeres. . . .
There filled with true light, with wondring eyes
The wandring planets, and fixt stars he sees.
He sees our day involv'd in midst of night,
And laughes at his torn trunkes ridiculous plight.

Like Arcita's flight, Pompey's ascent culminates in an act of
cognition. As medieval glosses explain, *vero lumine* denotes sa-
pience or divine knowledge, whereas the phrase *quanta sub nocte*
refers to human knowledge, which is folly in the sight of God.

---

spirit to heaven ascends. . . ." Cf. translation by Sir Arthur Gorges, *Lucans
Pharsalia* (London, 1614, HEH # 17266), pp. 358-359:

                 But yet the soule aloft aspires
                 And staied not in the *Pharian* fires. . . .
                 The base unworthy tombe it leaves,
                 The thundring vault the same receaves.
                 Whereas the duskie aire confines
                 Next to the orbes that lowest shines;
                 And where the distance spacious
                 Is spread between the Moone and us.
                 Where soules and demi-gods doe dwell,
                 Whose shining vertues did excell:
                 And upright lives did them prepare,
                 In this low element to share.
                 Whereas his blessed ghost it reares
                 To rest in the eternall spheres. . . .
                 And when he was in this faire seate
                 With ioyous perfect light repleat;
                 He viewes the wandring starres in skies,
                 And fixed planets Markes likewise:
                 And sees (in value of that light)
                 Our brightest dayes are but as night.
                 And of those scornes he makes but mirth,
                 That they doe to his Trunke on earth.

Arcita, in turn, similarly condemns the "tenebrosa cechitate" of humanity, "Mattamente oscurati nelle menti. . . ."[9]

From the *Pharsalia* let us turn to the *Commedia*. In the twenty-second canto of the *Paradiso*, Dante attains the heaven of the fixed stars and for the first time beholds the entire planetary system—the earth and the seven spheres centered upon it—in a single view:[10]

> 'Tu se' sì presso a l' ultima salute,'
>   Cominciò Beatrice, 'che tu dei
>   Aver le luci tue chiare ed acute.
> E però, prima che tu più t' inlei,
>   Rimira in giù, e vedi quanto mondo
>   Sotto li piedi già esser ti fei. . . .'
> Col viso ritornai per tutte quante
>   Le sette spere, e vidi questo globo
>   Tal, ch' io sorrisi del suo vil sembiante;
> E quel consiglio per migliore approbo
>   Che l' ha per meno; e chi ad altro pensa
>   Chiamar si puote veramente probo.

"Thou art so nigh to the supreme weal," began Beatrice, "that thou shouldst have thine eyes clear and keen. And therefore, ere thou further wend thereinto, look down and see how great a universe I have already put beneath thy feet. . . ."

With my sight I turned back through all and every of the seven spheres, and saw this globe such that I smiled at its sorry semblance; and that counsel I approve as best which holdeth it for least; and he whose thoughts are turned elsewhither may be called truly upright.[11]

The flight scenes of Lucan, Dante, and Boccaccio not only center on similar clusters of commonplaces—ascent to the heavens, contemplation of the planets, a turning backward to regard the earth, and a comparison between terrene and celestial values, culminating in an outburst of laughter—but also contain minor verbal parallels. Taken individually, some of these seem too

---

[9] Cf. Giovanni Boccaccio, *Teseida. Delle Nozze d' Emilia*, ed. Aurelio Roncaglia (Bari, 1941), p. 316.

[10] Dante Alighieri, *La Divina Commedia*, ed. C. H. Grandgent, rev. ed. (Boston, 1933), p. 863 (hereafter cited as Grandgent).

[11] Dante Alighieri, *The Divine Comedy*, the Carlyle-Okey-Wicksteed translation (New York, n.d.), pp. 541-542 (hereafter cited as Carlyle-Wicksteed).

tenuous to serve as reliable evidence. Taken as a whole, however, they may strengthen the probability that we are dealing with a continuous and closely linked tradition—a pattern of influences extending from the *Pharsalia* through the *Paradiso* to the *Teseida*, and thence to the *Troilus*. Pompey admires the planets and fixed stars; "stellasque vagas miratus et astra Fixa polis. . . ." Both Dante and Boccaccio drop the fixed stars but retain the admiration of the planets. Boccaccio's line "quivi le stelle ratiche ammirava" is closer to Lucan than to Dante, who merely refers to the planets as "Le sette spere" and transfers the verb *mirare* to a different line. In two minor details, however, we may observe verbal parallels with Dante. Though they may be merely fortuitous, we must mention them in justice to those critics who emphasize the influence of the *Paradiso* on the *Teseida*. Boccaccio's lines "Quindi si volse in giù a rimirare le cose abandonate" may conceivably echo Beatrice's command, "Rimira in giù, e vedi quanto mondo Sotto li piedi già esser ti fei. . . ." Similarly, Boccaccio's phrase "vide il poco globo terreno" is closer to Dante's "vidi questo globo" than to Lucan's "vidit quanta sub nocte Nostra dies. . . ."[12]

Arcita's laughter at the laments of the mob ("e seco rise de' pianti dolenti della turba lernea") seems closer to Pompey's laughter at the fate of his remains ("risitque sui ludibria trunci") than to Dante's mirth at the spectacle of the "vile" world ("Tal, ch'io sorrisi del suo vil sembiante").

Other *topoi* in Boccaccio's stanzas have no close parallel in the flight passages of Lucan and Dante. For the most part, however, they are commonplaces, and we need not look for a particular

---

[12] For further discussion of these verbal parallels, see Clark, "Dante and the Epilogue," pp. 4-5. Patch, "Chauceriana," p. 359, declares that "Chaucer's phrase 'the blinde lust' doubtless reflects Boccaccio's 'tenebrosa cechitate.'" For the relationship between the "blynde lust," of the epilogue, the "blynde entencioun" of Book I, line 211, the phrase "blynde thoght" in Chaucer's translation of Boethius, and Boccaccio's allusion to *cecità* in Book I, stanza 25 of *Il Filostrato*, see P. M. Kean, "Chaucer's Dealing with a Stanza of *Il Filostrato* and the Epilogue of *Troilus and Criseyde*," *Medium AEvum*, XXXIII (1964), 36-46.

source. After alluding in his first stanza to the convex of the elements ("degli elementi i convessi"), Boccaccio proceeds to amplify this allusion in the following stanza, listing in succession earth, sea, air, and fire. The Dantesque analogue does not refer to the elements at all, and Lucan himself alludes merely to the conjunction of air and aether.

Though Boccaccio's allusion to the small size of the earth ("il poco globo terreno") has numerous parallels in Boethius and Cicero and in astronomical treatises, there are no close analogues in the passages usually adduced from the *Paradiso* and the *Pharsalia*. To be sure, Dante does indeed allude to the globe's "vil sembiante," approving the view that holds it "per meno." The latter phrase, however, can be taken in a qualitative as well as a quantitative sense. Grandgent construes it as meaning "holds it cheapest."[13] Dante's line may, however, underlie another passage in Boccaccio's stanza: "e ogni cosa da nulla stimare a rispetto del ciel. . . ." Chaucer's translation, "this litel spot of erthe, that with the se Enbraced is," slightly alters Boccaccio's lines by substituting "spot" for "globe" and suppressing the reference to the elements of air and fire. In this way he brings the passage into closer conformity with the tradition he could have encountered in *Scipio's Dream* and in Boethius's *De Consolatione*: earth as a point or *punctum* in comparison with the heavens, and the inhabitable lands themselves as a mere point in comparison with the surrounding sea.

Boccaccio's allusion to the music of the spheres has no parallel in Lucan's account of Pompey or in Dante's view of the earth. Dante has encountered the celestial harmony long before, while passing through the sphere of fire. Though this detail also occurs in the *Somnium Scipionis*, there is little reason to seek a specific source for Boccaccio's reference to this commonplace.

Though scholars are correct in recognizing Boccaccio's dual indebtedness to Lucan and Dante, we have (it would seem) little justification for emphasizing one over the other as his "principal" source. In certain respects the *Teseida* stanzas show a closer

---

[13] Grandgent, p. 863n.

resemblance to the *Pharsalia*; in other details, however, they seem nearer to the twenty-second canto of the *Paradiso*. As Dante himself appears to have been influenced by Lucan, Boccaccio would have been indirectly indebted to the Roman author through the Florentine. Parallels in literary context, *topoi*, and phrasing also suggest, however, the direct influence of the *Pharsalia*. Pompey's flight and Dante's ascent belong to the same literary tradition. In his account of Arcita's soul, Boccaccio has effectively combined elements from both authors—from Dante and from at least one of Dante's sources.

2

From this preliminary comparison of analogues, let us return to the problem of the eighth sphere. On this point comparative studies of Boccaccio's sources will not help us much. Whether the primary influence on the flight stanzas was Lucan (as Scott argues), Cicero (as Root believed), or Dante (as Dobson maintains), Boccaccio has clearly altered or combined, omitted or supplemented many of the details he encountered in these authors. His adaptations of Dante and Lucan show a considerable degree of selectivity, and he may have felt equally free to choose Arcita's destination. After all, Dante had exercised comparable freedom of choice in combining and altering details derived from Lucan and Cicero. Moreover, there is always the possibility that Boccaccio's ambiguity may have been deliberate—a conscious refusal to choose between Lucan, on the one hand, and Dante and Cicero, on the other. Nor will medieval traditions concerning the celestial habitations of great men solve the problem. The traditions themselves were often at variance, and commentators were frequently hard put to reconcile them. The text of Boccaccio's alleged sources—and medieval or Renaissance commentaries on them—may lend limited assistance, but in the final analysis the answer must be sought in Boccaccio's own lines.

In the *Teseida*, Arcita's light spirit ("anima leve") leaves the convexes of the elements in its ascent toward the concave of the eighth sphere. This account retains the Aristotelian contrast between gravity and levity, but it also reflects a conventional scientific distinction between the elementary and ethereal parts of the world. According to John Holywood's treatise *De Sphaera*, "The machine of the universe is divided into two, the ethereal and the elementary region. The elementary region, existing subject to continual alteration, is divided into four. For there is earth, placed, as it were, in the center in the middle of all, about which is water, about water air, about air fire, which is pure and not turbid there and reaches to the sphere of the moon. . . . Three of them, in turn, surround the earth on all sides spherically, except in so far as the dry land stays the sea's tide. . . ." God has disposed them thus, and by turns the four elements are "altered, corrupted and regenerated." The elementary region is subject to change, but the "ethereal" region that revolves about it "is lucid and immune from all variation in its immutable essence." It comprises nine spheres, ranging from the moon and Mercury to the fixed stars and the "last heaven."[14]

Though recent scholarship has sought to demonstrate Chaucer's debt to Holywood's treatise,[15] we shall consider it primarily on other grounds. It is interesting not only as another possible source for the *Teseida* and the *Troilus*, but as a representative statement of the astronomical and meteorological concepts with which Boccaccio and Chaucer have amplified their materials. Holywood's distinction between the elementary region (which

[14] Lynn Thorndike, *The "Sphere" of Sacrobosco and Its Commentators* (Chicago, 1949), p. 119.

[15] Cf. S. W. Harvey, "Chaucer's Debt to Sacrobosco," *JEGP*, XXXIV (1935), 34-38; Walter B. Veazie, "Chaucer's Text-Book of Astronomy: Johannes de Sacrobosco," *University of Colorado Studies, Series B. Studies in the Humanities*, I (1940), 169-182. Among recent studies of Chaucer's use of astronomy and astrology, see Florence Marie Grimm, "Astronomical Lore in Chaucer," *University of Nebraska Studies in Language, Literature, and Criticism* (1919); Curry, *Chaucer and the Mediaeval Sciences*, pp. 245-265 and *passim*; Wood, "Chaucer and Astrology," in Rowland, *Companion to Chaucer Studies*; Wood, *Chaucer and the Country of the Stars*; Gustav Herdan, "Chaucer's Authorship of *The Equatorie of the Planetis*: The Use of Romance Vocabulary as Evidence," *Language*, XXXII (1956), 254-259; Derek J. Price, ed., *The Equatorie of the Planetis* (Cambridge, 1955).

extends to the moon) and the ethereal region (which extends from the moon to the last heaven) corresponds roughly to Lucan's distinction between the regions of air and aether, which meet at the lunar orbit ("lunaeque meatus"). After forsaking his body, Pompey's soul "sought the dome of the Thunderer" ("sequitur convexa Tonantis"). On the meaning of this passage early commentators expressed a variety of opinions. Papias's dictionary defined *convexa* as "extrema caeli flexa,"[16] and several expositors interpreted Lucan's phrase as a reference to the firmament. According to Arnulf of Orleans, Pompey's soul had ascended on high ("in altum") whence it had originally come: "Celum enim convexum est et incurvum." Following Neoplatonic doctrine, Arnulf described the two celestial gates, in Cancer and Capricorn, through which human souls descended to earth or returned to their own stars ("ad comparem stellam"). For souls (he explained) had been created in the same number as the stars, and each soul was nourished ("dicitur nutriri") together with its own star.

Echoing the Neoplatonic distinction between four kinds of virtues—political, purgatorial, purified, and exemplary—[17] Arnulf declared that the second and third categories did not linger in purgation after the dissolution of their bodies, but returned forthwith to their own stars. The souls of governors of commonwealths ("rectores urbium," like Pompey) belonged to the political virtues. After death they underwent a temporary period of purification in the air. Just as in descending they had lost a portion of divinity to each of the planets and assumed a corporeal nature, so in ascending they would discard the latter and recover their lost divinity. In seeking the convex of the Thunderer, Pompey's soul had fixed its intention on the Creator, following the "rational" movement of the firmament in contrast to the "irrational" motion

[16] Papias, *Vocabularium* (Venetiis, 1496, HEH # 103798), *s.v. convexa*. Professor Marti dates Papias's work ca. 1063; see Berthe M. Marti, ed., *Arnulfi Aurelianensis glosule super Lucanum* (Rome, 1958), p. xxxiii. Cf. Arnulfus's commentary on *Pharsalia*, Book V. line 632 (Marti, p. 297), "CONVEXA id est sphere planetarum . . . ."

[17] Cf. *Somnium Scipionis* (Stahl, pp. 121, 126) on the same fourfold classification of virtues and on the return of the soul to the fixed stars.

of the planets. For to "follow the firmament" is simply to despise all earthly things (*terrena*) and to direct intention toward the Creator alone.[18]

For Arnulf, then, the term *convexa Tonantis* denoted the firmament. Nevertheless, he explicitly denied that Pompey himself had attained this region: "et ne ex hoc quod dixit SEQUITUR CONVEXA TONANTIS credatur statim venisse ad ipsum firmamentum, subiungit: qua ether iungitur aeri. . . ."[19]

Similar interpretations appear in another medieval commentary on the *Pharsalia*, now in the Biblioteca Medicea-Laurenziana in Florence. Since this manuscript (according to Professor Berthe Marti) "may have belonged to Boccaccio,"[20] its glosses possess a special interest in spite of their brevity. Like several other expositors, this author apparently interpreted the third and fourth lines (*Prosiluit . . . sequitur convexa Tonantis*) as an indication that the flight of Pompey's soul followed the rational movement

[18] Marti, *Arnulfi*, p. xlviii, notes a parallel in Hugh of Saint Victor's account of rational and irrational motions.

[19] Marti, *Arnulfi*, pp. 431-434. Professor Marti observes (p. xxxiii) that Arnulf was "deeply influenced" by the school of Chartres and contemporary Neoplatonists and that much of his information on the nature of the world "seems to have been compiled from Macrobius's *Somnium Scipionis* . . . , with additions borrowed, either directly or indirectly, from Chalcidius, Martianus Capella, Pliny and others" (p. xlv). For bibliographical references to studies of Arnulf's glosses and other medieval commentaries on Lucan, see Marti, *Arnulfi*, pp. xxx-xxxi. Cf. Marti, "Literary Criticism in the Mediaeval Commentaries on Lucan," *Transactions of the American Philological Association*, LXXII (1941), 245-254; Marti, "Lucan's Invocation to Nero in the Light of the Mediaeval Commentaries," *Quadrivium*, I (1956), 7-18; Eva M. Sanford, "The Manuscripts of Lucan: Accessus and Marginalia," *Speculum*, IX (1934), 278-295; *M. Annaei Lucani Pharsalia*, ed. C. F. Weber (Lipsiae, 1821-1831), *passim*..

[20] Codex Laur. Plut. 35. 23, c. In "Vacca in Lucanum," *Speculum*, XXV (1950), 203, Marti observes that the manuscript contains "glosses borrowed mostly from Anselm of Laon." On the commentary attributed to Anselm, see Marti, *Arnulfi . . . glosule*, pp. xxxi-xxxii. See also Max Manitius, *Geschichte der lateinischen Literatur des Mittelalters* (München, 1931), III, 238. For a listing of Lucan MSS by country, see Manitius, "Handschrift antiker Autoren in mittelalterlichen Bibliothekskatalogen," ed. Karl Manitius, *Zentralblatt für Bibliothekswesen* (Leipzig, 1935), LXVII, 115-120.

of the firmament, the sphere of the fixed stars. In this respect Lucan's hero had demonstrated his superiority to the other political rulers: "alii urbium rectores saliunt. sed iste porro saliet imitatus aplanon." The term "convex" referred to the curving heavens (*caelum . . . inclinum*). Nevertheless, Pompey's spirit did not ascend immediately to the firmament, and to prevent this misconception ("ne putareris eam statim ad ipsum venisse firmamentum"), Lucan has specified the point to which Pompey's *manes* actually had ascended: the region where the misty and dense air ("iste haer crassus et spissus") joins the moon and the other planets. The same commentator explains the phrase . . . *et aeternos animam collegit in orbes* as an allusion to the contrast between the temporal and eternal movements of reason: "& collegit animam. quae prius erat sparsa in mundanis. in eternos horbes .i. nunc in motum rationis eternalem. quae prius in motum rationis temporalem erat."[21]

Another medieval commentator specifically identified the habitation of the *semidei manes* as the lunar circle: "lunaris circulus qui est inferior omnibus circulis . . .inter summum aeris nigri et imum aetheris."[22]

Several Renaissance commentators not only assigned Pompey's soul to the lunar orb but insisted that Lucan's term *convexa* really meant the "concave" of the heavens. According to Giovanni Sulpizio of Veroli, "sequitur convexa" signified "repetit caeli concavitatem."[23] In the opinion of Iodocus Badius Ascensius, this phrase denoted "caeli aut aetheris (nam summus aer Iuppiter est) concavitatem. . . ."[24] Filippo Beroaldo explained that "Umbra Pompeij petijt coelum qua parte aer summus connectitur circulo lunari qui aer purus est & liquidus & imperturbatae lucis ut aiunt

---

[21] Codex Laur. Plut. 35. 23, c. 77v. I am indebted to the Director of the Biblioteca Medicea-Laurenziana for permission to quote from this manuscript and for a photograph of the relevant passage.

[22] Hermannus Usener, ed., *Scholia in Lucani Bellum Civile Pars Prior . . . Commenta Bernensia* (Lipsaie, 1968), p. 289.

[23] *Lucanus cum duobus commentis* (Mediolani, 1499, HEH # 90997).

[24] *M. Annei Lucani . . . Pharsalia diligentissime per G. Versellanum recognita* (Paris, 1514, HEH # 349571), fol. ccxv.

Cicero & Plinius."[25] One commentator—Ognibuono di Lonigo—maintained that Pompey's soul was seeking its own star: "Sequitur convexa tonantis: revertitur ad comparem stellam & ad caeleste domicilium." Temporarily, however, his spirit must remain among the heroes below the moon: "nunc autem dicit non posse, quidem animam ad summam aeterem ascendere: sed in medio terrarum ac lunae suum domicilium habere."[26]

Until additional commentaries on the *Pharsalia* have been published, we must defer judgment on the relation of these Renaissance expositors to their medieval predecessors. From the limited material available to us, however, their divergent interpretations seem to derive partly from the conflict between different eschatological traditions and partly from the ambiguity of Lucan's terminology. If interpreted as the *convex* of the heavens, the phrase *convexa Tonantis* would apparently denote the firmament. If construed as meaning the *concave* of the heavens, however, Lucan's phrase would apparently refer to the lunar circle. The latter interpretation would be more consonant with the lines immediately following, in which Lucan describes the abode of the heroes. It is significant that, even though Arnulf prefers the former reading, he expressly assigns Pompey to the lunar sphere.

Lucan's ambiguity puzzled his commentators, just as the ambiguity of Boccaccio and Chaucer perplexes their expositors today. In both cases, curiously enough, the controversy has tended to center on the same celestial alternatives: the lunar concave or the sphere of the fixed stars. Conceivably, the divergence of Boccaccio and Dante on this point may reflect not only the disagreement of classical poets and philosophers as to the habitations of the dead but also the disagreement of Lucan's own expositors.

We should note, moreover, a further analogy between Boccaccio and Chaucer, on the one hand, and Lucan's commentators, on the other. Lucan's expositors usually agree in placing Pompey

---

[25] *Ibid.*, fol ccxv.
[26] *Lucanus cum duobus commentis.*

temporarily in the lunar concave,[27] among the heroes. They sometimes disagree, however, as to whether this will be his ultimate destination; a few insist that he will ultimately return to his own star (*ad comparem stellam*), even though Lucan depicts him as returning to earth to seek revenge. Chaucer and Boccaccio send their heroes temporarily to the concave of the moon, but sidestep the problem of their final habitation, leaving the resolution to Mercury.

Boccaccio's allusion to the "concavity" of the eighth sphere may have been influenced by scholarly glosses that identified Lucan's *convexa Tonantis* with the concave of the heavens. The idea is a commonplace, however, and there is little point in seeking a specific source. Boccaccio's reference to the "convexes" of the *elements* has no close parallel in the published commentaries on the *Pharsalia*. It is, however, an accurate term for the spherical layers of elements as conceived by medieval cosmology. Boccaccio's picture of the round earth embraced by the sea and encompassed by the gyres of air and fire represents the well-established notion of the "concaves" of the four elements, but seen (significantly) from above.

3

Though Boccaccio is quite explicit about the spheres of the elementary region through which Arcita has passed, he does not describe a comparable flight through the spheres of the ethereal region. In the absence of contrary evidence, the juxtaposition of lines on the "convexes" of the elements and the "concavity" of the eighth sphere might suggest that the latter should be identified with the moon. The "concave of the moon" was a conventional astronomical term for the utmost limits of the elementary region and the lower limits of the ethereal, and at least one commentator on Holywood's treatise introduced it into his account of the

---

[27] Housman places Pompey in the lunar circle, citing parallels in Chryssippus, Porphyry, Plutarch, Sextus Empiricus, Cicero, Tertullian, and Servius; A. E. Housman, ed., *M. Annaei Lucani Belli Civilis Libri Decem* (Cambridge, Mass., 1926), p. 255n.

concentric layers of elements. According to Cecco d'Ascoli,[28] "elementaris machina subiecta est continue transmutationi que dividitur in quatuor elementa, quia terra est tanquam centrum in medio posita, circa quam est aqua, circa aquam est aer, circa aerem est ignis, illic purus non turbidus attingens concavum lune . . . et ut dicit Aristoteles *in libro Metheororum*, Sic disposuit deus sublimis et gloriosus." The same author also found a direct relationship between the form of the lunar concave and the convexities of the elements. Like water in a vase, "corpus contentum a concavo orbis lune oportet esse orbiculare." Another commentator on *De Sphaera*, Michael Scot, drew the same correlation in similar terms: the elements derived their circular form from that of the lunar concave: "per accidens igitur figurantur a concavo lune, scilicet ignis et aer a concavo ignis, terra vero rotunda est in centrum, tamen quia locatum a concavo aque. . . ."[29]

Just as these astronomical writers correlated the "concaves" of the elements with the lunar concave, Boccaccio contrasts the convexes of the elements with the concave of the eighth sphere. In this detail Chaucer may have followed him, for (in Root's opinion) Chaucer's *convers* may be an error for *convess*.[30] The fact that Boccaccio refers to the "convexes" of the elements rather than to their "concaves" does not appreciably alter this astronomical commonplace. It merely underlines the fact that Arcita's soul has passed *above* the elements, but *not* above the eighth sphere. The terms *convex* and *concave* are frequently used almost synonymously, but in the strictest sense they refer respectively to the exterior and interior surfaces of a sphere.[31] Thus according to Robertus Anglicus,[32] there are three sorts of surfaces or

[28] Thorndike, *The "Sphere,"* p. 357.

[29] *Ibid.*, p. 294.

[30] Root, *The Book of Troilus and Criseyde*, p. 561.

[31] Cf. Mahmoud Manzalaoui, "Roger Bacon's *In Convexitate* and Chaucer's *In Convers* (*Troilus and Criseyde* V. 1810)," *Notes and Queries*, n.s., XI (1964), 165-166.

[32] Thorndike, *The "Sphere,"* p. 145.

superficies. One is flat, like the surface of a parchment; another is concave, like the interior surface of an onion; the third is convex, like the exterior surface of an apple. Similar distinctions are made by Michael Scot and anonymous commentators on *De Sphaera*.[33]

Against this background of astronomical and meteorological doctrine, it seems reasonable to infer that Arcita has reached the concave of the moon. The spatial and temporal sequence of his observation, moreover, supports this inference. After admiring the planets and listening to their music, Arcita *turns* and looks *backward* upon the earth and its encompassing elements: "quindi si volse in giù a rimirare Le cose abandonate. . . ." This movement suggests that he is located below the planets rather than above them.[34] If he had actually reached the fixed stars, he

---

[33] *Ibid.*, pp. 256, 414, 456-457.

[34] On these grounds Clark argues ("Dante and the Epilogue," pp. 6-8) that Boccaccio "very clearly implies that Arcita's station, when he looked down upon the earth, was in the lunar sphere," but that "Chaucer's picture" may be "intentionally" ambiguous. Clark does "not think that Chaucer misunderstood Boccaccio or wished to depart from him clearly and definitely in the choice of a station for his hero's retrospective ghost. . . ." Like Professor Clark, I feel that it is unlikely that Chaucer misunderstood Boccaccio. Nevertheless just how far Chaucer's ambiguity was intentional must remain a matter for speculation. Boccaccio's allusions to Elysium (which will be considered in the next chapters), together with his account of Arcita's turning back to regard the earth, seem to identify his *concavità* of the eighth heaven with the lunar concave. Although Troilus's precise situation is less clear, the weight of the evidence seems, in my opinion, to support a similar interpretation. In the first place, allusions to the concave (or "holughnesse") of the moon are far more common in astronomical treatises than references to the concave of the firmament (or *aplanes*). In contrast with numerous references to the *convex* of the firmament, allusions to its *concave* are rare. Second, Chaucer describes Troilus as leaving the elementary region behind him—a flight that would bring him to the lunar concave—but does not describe a further ascent through the spheres. Though he beholds the planets and hears the music of the spheres, the text does not provide the slightest suggestion that he is passing (or has passed) through them. Third, it is at this point—immediately after leaving the region of the elements—that Troilus is described as looking down upon the earth; even though Chaucer does not allude specifically to the act of turning, the downward glance occurs, significantly, *after*—not before—the vision of the heavens. In this respect Troilus's closest affinities are with Arcita rather than with Dante.

would have been compelled to turn and look *downward* to contemplate the planets, and in doing so he would have comprehended the earth in the same view. This (as we recall) was Dante's action: "Col viso ritornai per tutte quante Le sette spere, e vidi questo globo. . . ." The greater part of the universe lay under Dante's feet. Arcita's situation is different. He does *not* turn to regard the planetary spheres, but he *is* compelled to turn back in order to contemplate the elements and the earthly globe. Here again, his situation bears a closer resemblance to Pompey's than to Dante's.[35]

---

[35] As the moon is almost certainly Arcita's immediate end—and possibly Troilus's stopping-place as well—we should also consider the problem of Chaucer's eighth sphere in relation to the theme of constancy and inconstancy in his poem. On the one hand, to identify the eighth sphere with the stellar firmament would provide a more forceful contrast between celestial steadfastness and earthly mutability. The lunar interpretation, on the other hand, could symbolically introduce the theme of inconstancy in Troilus's ascent. He would then appear, like the former nuns in Dante's lunar paradise, to have merited a lesser reward for not having been altogether constant to the supreme Good. As Grandgent observes (p. 741), Saint Thomas Aquinas, in his commentary on Aristotle's *Metaphysics*, "ascribes to the various planets certain dominant effects, which to some extent correspond to the attributes selected by Dante. Stability . . . is characteristic of Saturn; mutability, of the moon." The moon is further associated, not only with inconstancy, but with the voluptuous life and "incipient Charity." (cf. *ibid.,* pp. 651, 674-5, 683.) It would therefore be an appropriate destination for a hero whose bliss and double sorrow have been consistently conceived and represented in terms of the *vita voluptaria*.

CHAPTER II

"FIELD OF PITE":
ELYSIUM AND PURGATORY

Perhaps good Americans still go to Paris when they die, but this is a subject for epigram, not for eschatology. Where good heroes and pagan worthies went was a controversial question, even in antiquity, and Christian divines held protracted debates on the matter. Homer's Menelaos could look forward to perpetual happiness in the Elysian plain at the "farthest borders of the earth . . . where dwells fair-haired Rhadamanthys," but he owed his exceptionally good fortune to an advantageous marriage: he was the "son-in-law of Zeus."[1] Hesiod's golden and silver races became daimons, guardians respectively of mankind and of the underworld; the men of bronze, in their turn, descended unhonored to Hades. Of the heroes of Thebes and Troy, however, some passed immediately to the islands of the blessed beside the river Oceanus to enjoy three harvests a year.[2] To this region Pindar assigned Peleus, Kadmos, and Achilles. With later writers the inhabitants of Elysium became still more numerous; they included Diomedes and Neoptolemos, Agamemnon and Alkmene, and (that they might not want eloquence to extol their merits) Demosthenes. If the orator seems perhaps an alien intruder in this society of heroes, we should recall that Rhadmanthys, possibly the first sojourner in the Greek Elysium, was primarily distinguished for his justice and that Plato had suggested an etymological link between the hero and the orator. For some of

[1] W. K. C. Guthrie, *The Greeks and Their Gods* (Boston, 1955), p. 290.

[2] Erwin Rohde, *Psyche, the Cult of Souls and Belief in Immortality Among the Greeks*, trans. W. B. Hillis (New York, 1966), I, 67-68. According to Quintus of Smyrna, Achilles's *manes* "leaped up like a swift breeze, and straightway came to the Elysian plain, where is made a way of descent from highest Heaven and ascent for the blessed Immortals"; Guthrie, *Orpheus and Greek Religion* (New York, 1966), p. 208.

the ancients, even Elysium seemed an insufficient remuneration for Demosthenes; accordingly, they elevated him into an attendant *daimon* on Zeus Eleutherios.

Virgil, in turn, converted Elysium into a sort of "suburb eternal" of the *urbs aeterna*, filling its spacious meadows and airy fields (*aeris in campis latis*) with noble Romans. Here, as if aestivating in the Campagna, they enjoyed a spectral *fête champêtre* in the company of their Trojan ancestors, with a select group of poets to entertain them. Like the surface of the earth, the underworld had also become Roman; even the Elysian fields had been annexed as a subterranean province of the empire.

1

From the fables of the poets let us turn to the speculations and parables of the philosophers. According to Plato's *Timaeus*, "the author of this universe" had created "souls equal in number with the stars, and distributed them, each soul to its several star. There mounting them as it were in chariots, he showed them the nature of the universe and declared to them the laws of Destiny. There would be appointed a first incarnation one and the same for all. . . And he who should live well for his due span of time should journey back to the habitation of his consort star and there live a happy and congenial life; but failing of this, he should shift at his second birth into a woman; and if in this condition he did not cease from wickedness, then according to the character of his depravation, he should constantly be changed into some beast of a nature resembling the formation of that character. . . ."[3]

In the *Phaedo* Socrates had painted a glowing picture of the "upper earth" which awaits the purified soul: "And upon the earth are animals and men, some in a middle region, others dwelling about the air as we dwell about the sea, others in islands which the air flows round, near the continent: and in a word, the

[3] Francis M. Cornford, trans., *Plato's Timaeus*, ed. Oskar Piest (Indianapolis and New York, 1959), pp. 37-38.

air is used by them, as the water and the sea are by us, and the ether is to them what the air is to us." The abodes of souls purified by philosophy surpassed speech.[4] The myth of Er in the *Republic*[5] had described a meadow where souls ascended or descended through openings in heaven and earth. The *Phaedrus* had employed the image of the chariot to describe the symbolic journey of the soul about the heavens in contemplation of the Ideas. And in the *Gorgias* Socrates had explicitly linked the journey of man's soul after death with divine judgment and the allocation of rewards and punishments. There were "two ways" leading to the islands of the blessed and to Tartarus: "Now in the time of Cronos there was a law concerning mankind, and it holds to this very day amongst the gods, that every man who has passed a just and holy life departs after his decease to the Isles of the Blest, and dwells in all happiness apart from ill; but whoever has lived unjustly and impiously goes to . . . Tartarus." Unlike Socrates' own judges, the magistrates who conducted the post-mortem inquest on the soul showed a pronounced bias in favor of philosophers. For when Rhadamanthys discerned a "soul that has lived a holy life in company with truth . . . —especially . . . a philosopher's who has . . . not been a busybody in his life-time—he is struck with admiration and sends it off to the Isles of the Blest."[6]

With Plato, Elysium had become virtually a supramundane Academy, preeminently the abode of the preeminently purified —the philosophers. With the Neoplatonists this tendency became still more marked. According to Philo, the highest station in the ether belonged to the purest souls: the sages who had introduced philosophy into Greece and were honored after death as heroes and daimons. Plotinus similarly defined heroic virtue as the virtue

---

[4] *The Works of Plato*, trans. Benjamin Jowett (New York, n.d.), III, 262, 266.

[5] *Ibid.*, II, 407-408.

[6] *Plato*, trans. W. R. M. Lamb, Loeb Classical Library (London and New York, 1925), V, 519-529.

of a purified soul.[7] Amplifying Pythagorean and Platonic conceptions of the descent and reascent of the soul, he argued that
"since each soul, as a microcosm, contains within itself a representation not only of the whole intelligible world, but also of the
soul which guides the visible universe, it may find itself, after the
departure from the body, in the sun or one or more of the planets
or in the sphere of the fixed stars, according as it has energised
with the power related to this or that part of the whole. Those
souls that have overpassed the 'daemonic nature' are at this stage
of their mutation outside all destiny of birth and beyond the
limits of the visible heaven."[8] Porphyry's *Sententiae* in turn
achieved a "systematic classification" of the virtues that would
recur in medieval and Renaissance speculations on the purification and reascent of the soul, "Political, Cathartic, Theoretic

[7] Cf. John M. Steadman, *Milton's Epic Characters* (Chapel Hill, N.C.,
1968), pp. 320, 328. Like the heroes, the daimons were sometimes assigned to
the air under the moon. According to Martin P. Nilsson, *Greek Piety*, trans.
Herbert Jennings Rose (New York, 1969), p. 89, "one of Plato's successors,
Xenokrates . . . looked up certain hints in Plato concerning daimones as
intermediate beings between gods and men and built on to them. The
daimones have their abode in the air, under the moon; their nature is a
combination of the divine, the spiritual, and the corporeal. . . ." Cf. Nilsson, *A
History of Greek Religion*, trans. F. J. Fielden, 2d ed. (New York, 1964), pp.
289-290. (Traditionally the daimons constituted a higher order than the heroes
and occupied a higher region in the skies; cf. Steadman, *Milton's Epic
Characters*, pp. 319-330.) In *Orpheus and Greek Religion* (p. 193), Nilsson
observes that Plutarch's *De facie in orbe lunae* represents the moon as "an
intermediate stage in the upward progress of the soul." Calling attention to the
"mingling of mythological and philosophical expression, as seen . . . in the
fitting of the ancient Elysium into a cosmological scheme by placing it in the
moon," Nilsson cites W. Hamilton's summary (*Classical Quarterly*, XXVIII
[1934], 26) of the doctrine that after death the mind and soul "fly up to the
space between the earth and the moon, where they are punished and purified.
The moon receives after purification the souls of the just; there they enjoy the
delights of paradise . . . and there finally, if they do not by sin incur the
punishment of reincarnation, the second death takes place. Mind returns to the
sun, which was its source."

[8] Thomas Whittaker, *The Neo-Platonists*, 2d. ed. (Cambridge, 1928), p. 97;
cf. pp. 66, 73, 80-81, 166, 307; see also Raymond Klibansky, *The Continuity of
the Platonic Tradition During the Middle Ages* (London, 1939).

and Paradigmatic." Whereas political virtues "set the soul free
from excess of passionate attachment to the body, and produce
moderation," cathartic virtues "liberate it altogether from this
attachment, so that it can now turn to its true good." The third
group comprises "virtues of the soul energising intellectually,"
while the fourth class consists of patterns that exist "in intellect
itself."[9]

Though the Stoics held diverse views concerning the fate of
the soul, Arnold suggests that "on certain points all Stoic teachers
seem to be agreed: first, that the soul is, as regards its substance,
imperishable; secondly, that the individual soul cannot survive the
general conflagration; lastly, that it does not of necessity perish
with the body." Since the soul is compounded of air and fire it
must "by its own nature, when freed from the body, pierce
through this murky atmosphere, and rise to a brighter region
above, let us say to that sphere which is just below the moon.
Here . . . souls dwell like the stars, finding like them their food in
exhalations from the earth. Here they take rank as daemons or
heroes. . . ."[10] According to Diogenes Laertius, the Stoics believed
in daimons who "are in sympathy with mankind and watch
over human affairs" and in heroes, "the souls of the righteous
[σπουδαίων] that have survived their bodies."[11] They regarded
wise men as godlike [θείους] since these "have a something divine
within them."[12] Though they defined the soul as a body that
survived death and believed the soul of the universe to be
indestructible, they regarded individual souls as perishable. Nevertheless, they differed as to when and how these perished.
Whereas Cleanthes "holds that all souls continue to exist until the
general conflagration. . . Chrysippus says that only the souls of
the wise do so."[13]

---

[9] Klibansky, *Continuity*, p. 111.
[10] E. Vernon Arnold, *Roman Stoicism* (Cambridge, 1911), pp. 263-264.
[11] Diogenes Laertius, *Lives of Eminent Philosophers*, trans. R. D. Hicks,
Loeb Classical Library (London and New York, 1925), II, 255.
[12] *Ibid.,* II, 223.
[13] *Ibid.*, II, 261.

The first dialogue in Cicero's *Tusculan Disputations*—"De contemnenda morte"—raises the question of the immortality of the soul, arguing that death cannot be evil since it must "either render us happy if our souls survive, or free from wretchedness if we are without sensation."[14] Since by the principle of levity, the two light elements "fly vertically upward into the heavenly region," it is clear that "souls, on quitting the body, whether they are airy . . . or fiery, are carried aloft."[15] If the soul belongs to one of the four elements, it surely "consists of kindled air [*ex inflammata anima constat*] . . . and such a soul necessarily strives to reach higher regions. . . ."[16] There is, Cicero continues, "no sort of speed which can match the speed of the soul. If it survives unadulterated . . . it is of necessity carried away so rapidly as to pierce and part asunder all this atmosphere of ours, in which clouds, storms and winds collect. . . . When the soul has passed this tract and reaches to and recognizes a substance resembling its own, it stops amongst the fires which are formed of rarefied air and the modified glow of the sun and ceases to make higher ascent."[17] Whether the soul "is breath or fire, it is divine."[18] From the *Phaedo*, Cicero has borrowed Plato's fable of the "two paths . . . for souls on departure from the body: for those . . . who had polluted themselves with . . . sins . . . and delivered themselves over wholly to their lusts . . . had before them a road apart, remote from the company of the gods; they, on the other hand, who had kept themselves pure and chaste, who had suffered least contact with the body and always separated themselves from it and in the bodies of men had followed the life of the gods, had an easy way of return. . . ."[19]

During the period of the "Roman principate," Arnold ob-

---

[14] Cicero, *Tusculan Disputations.*, trans. J. E. King, Loeb Classical Library (Cambridge, Mass., and London, 1966), p. 31.

[15] *Ibid.*, p. 49.

[16] *Ibid.*, p. 51.

[17] *Ibid.*, p. 53.

[18] *Ibid.*, p. 71.

[19] *Ibid.*, p. 85.

serves, "the question of the future existence of the soul acquires special prominence." The writings of Seneca reflect the "accepted Stoic creed"—belief in a period of purgation after death, in the "life of pure souls in the regions of the aether," and in "final union with the divine being. It is after purgation that the soul by the refinement of the elements of which it is built forces its way to the higher regions; it finds a quiet and peaceful home in the clear bright aether; it has cast off the burden of the flesh; . . . it gazes on the human world below, and on the sublime company of the stars in its own neighborhood."[20]

In his Moral Epistles and Consolations, Seneca stresses the role of philosophy in liberating the soul by bidding it contemplate the universe and by directing it from earthly to divine things: *à terrenis ad divina*. One of the chief consolations for approaching death and a primary inducement to virtuous life is the fuller comprehension of nature's secrets that the righteous soul will achieve after death. The natural philosopher will consummate his contemplation of nature (*naturae rerum*) in the heavens themselves.

Renewing "its life in heaven" (Seneca maintains), the soul, "imprisoned as it has been in this gloomy and darkened house, seeks the open sky . . . and in contemplation of the universe finds rest."[21] Like Cato, the magnanimous man (*magnus animus*) complies with God's will, submitting to "whatever fate the law of the universe ordains." For at death the soul either returns to the universe to be mingled with nature, or dwells among divine things "amid greater radiance and calm."[22]

In another epistle Seneca contrasts the darkness of earthly ignorance with the light of celestial knowledge: "Our souls will not have reason to rejoice in their lot until, freed from this darkness in which they grope, they have not merely glimpsed the brightness with feeble vision, but have absorbed the full light of

[20] Arnold, *Roman Stoicism*, p. 268.
[21] Seneca, *Ad Lucilium Epistulae Morales*, trans. Richard M. Gummere, Loeb Classical Library (London and New York), I (1925), 453-455; Epistle 65.
[22] *Ibid.*, II (1920), 83; Epistle 71.

day and have been restored to their place in the sky—until . . . they have regained the place which they held at the allotment of their birth. The soul is summoned upward by its very origin. And it will reach that goal even before it is released from its prison below, as soon as it has cast off sin and, in purity and lightness, has leaped up into celestial realms of thought."[23] Again, in *To Polybius on Consolation*, Seneca declares that the soul, released from long imprisonment in the body and rejoicing to be at last its own master, "enjoys the spectacle of Nature, and from its higher place looks down upon all human things [*humana omnia ex loco superiore despicit*], while upon things divine, the explanation of which it had so long sought in vain, it gazes with a nearer vision [*divina vero . . . propius intuetur*]."[24]

Though the *Golden Verses of Pythagoras* placed the terrestrial daimons below the gods and heroes, classical tradition generally followed the Hesiodic hierarchy: gods, daimons, heroes, and men.[25] It was customary, therefore, to assign to the heroes a

[23] *Ibid.*, II, 207; Epistle 79. Cf. Epistle 102 (III, 180-181): "The human soul is a great and noble thing; it permits of no limits except those which can be shared even by the gods. . . . The soul's homeland [*patria*] is the whole space that encircles the height and breadth of the firmament, the whole rounded dome within which lie land and sea, within which the upper air that sunders the human from the divine also unites them, and where all the sentinel stars are taking their turn on duty [*quodcumque suprema et universa circuitu suo cingit, hoc omne convexum, intra quod iacent maria cum terris, intra quod aer humanis divinis secernens etiam coniungit, in quo disposita tot lumina in actus suos excubant*]. Again, the soul will not put up with a narrow span of existence."

[24] Seneca, *Moral Essays*, trans. John W. Basore, Loeb Classical Library (Cambridge, Mass., and London), II (1935), 378-381. The tradition that disembodied souls inhabit the pure air beneath the moon also recurs in Sextus Empiricus, whose *Adversus Mathematicos* (Antwerp, 1569, p. 271) repeats the argument that these are naturally carried upward by the levity of flame: "Nam cùm sint subtiles, & non minus igneae quam spirituales, sua levitate magis feruntur in loca superiora. . . . Cùm eae itaque fuerint extra Solis tabernaculum, habitant locum qui est sub Luna. & hic propter puritatem aëris accipiunt maius tempus ad permanendum: & utuntur alimento convenienti, nempe exhalatione ex terra, ut caetera astra."

[25] Cf. Steadman, *Milton's Epic Characters*, pp. 324-326.

region below the habitation of the gods and daimons. In the opinion of numerous writers, this was the lunar concave, though other authorities preferred the middle or lower regions of the air. In the alleged derivation of *heros* from words signifying air or earth, they found additional sanction for this view. Thus Saint Augustine records the belief that heroes derived their name from Juno (Hera) and dwelt in the air,[26] while Martianus Capella prefers the etymology from "earth": "Qui ex eo quod Heram Terram veteres dixerunt: Heroes nuncupati."[27] According to Augustine, Varro had placed the heroes immediately beneath the moon in the upper regions of the air: "The space betweene the highest heaven and the Moone he fills with soules ethereall and starres, affirming that they both are and seeme celestiall Gods; Betweene the Moone and the toppes of the windes he bestoweth ayry soules, but invisible (save to the mind) calling them *Heroes Lares*, and *Genij*."[28] Martianus assigns them to a lower station, *below* the middle regions of the air: "A medietate vero aeris usque in montium terraeque confinia Emithei: heroesque versantur. . . ." Accordingly, the heroes fall under the jurisdiction of Pluto, who rules the air beneath the moon and is called Summanus "quasi Summus Manium."[29]

If I have dwelt at length on these variations in classical pneumatology, it is because they are partly responsible for the variations that will be encountered in medieval commentaries on the *Pharsalia*. Though Homer, Hesiod, Pindar, and the greater part of Plato would have been inaccessible to the medieval glossators, they were not inaccessible to the classical and late classical Latin writers on whom the latter so frequently depended. Latin poetry and philosophy inherited the ambiguities and contradictions of their Greek prototypes, and these contrasts

---

[26] *Ibid.*, p. 328.

[27] *Martianus Capella de Nuptiis Philologiae et Mercurii* (Modena, 1500, HEH # 84875), Book II.

[28] Saint Augustine, *Of the City of God*, trans. John Healey (London, 1610, HEH # 98698), p. 264.

[29] Capella, Book II.

inevitably conditioned the differences as well as the similarities between Lucan and Cicero, Macrobius and Martianus. Some of the medieval commentators recognized a few of the divergences between Stoic and Platonic eschatology, and at least one of them courageously grappled with the problem of accommodating Lucan's predominantly Stoic pneumatology to a Neoplatonic frame of reference. These medieval reinterpretations of classical pneumatology are not readily comprehensible without a knowledge of their Greek as well as their Latin background. Nor (however limited his knowledge of the Greek tongue and his familiarity with Greek literature) is this background irrelevant to Boccaccio.

In varying degrees it was against this background that medieval and Renaissance commentators interpreted Lucan's flight passage and that one must approach the comparable scenes in Chaucer and Boccaccio. Both these authors seem to have consciously observed decorum (epic propriety as well as pagan verisimilitude) in elevating their respective heroes to a mythical Elysium—the abode of valiant heathen after death—and in assigning them a pagan divinity to conduct them to their new lodgings.

The immediate literary context of both these Elysium episodes will occupy us later. For the moment, let us turn to some of the medieval and Renaissance comments on Pompey's ascent, reexamining them in the light of the classical traditions we have already surveyed concerning Elysium and the reascent of the spirit.

2

Boccaccio's stanzas (as we have seen) apparently conduct Arcita to the lunar concave, where Pompey had ascended along before. This, in the opinion of many medieval or Renaissance exegetes, was one of several conventional sites of Elysium, and it is significant that Servius expounds Virgil's references to Elysium by quoting Lucan's account of Pompey's ascent. Observing that poets tended to locate Elysium in the underworld and philosophers to place it in the fortunate isles, Servius added that theologians situated it in the purer air of the lunar circle.[30] Through the prestige of Servius's commentary on the *Aeneid*, this definition became widely diffused during the Middle Ages and the Renaissance; Papias quoted it in his dictionary,[31] and it would reappear in later lexicons.

In commenting on *Aeneid* V, line 735 (*piorum concilia Elysiumque colo*), Servius turns to etymology and associates Elysium with absolution (i.e., separation of soul and body), citing (among other classical authors) Homer and Sallust, Porphyry and Lucan:[32]

. . . elysium est ubi piorum animae post corporis animaeque discretionem: . . . ergo elysium ἀπὸ τῆς λύσεως, *ab absolutione*: quod secundum poetas in medio inferorum est suis felicitatibus plenum, ut [VI, 641], *solemque suum sidera norunt.* secundum philosophos elysium est insulae fortunatae, quas ait Sallustius inclitas esse Homeri carminibus, quarum descriptionem Porphyrius commentator dicit esse sublatam: secundum theologos circa lunarem circulum, ubi iam aër purior est: unde ait ipse Vergilius [VI, 887] *aëris in campis*, item

[30] In the *Aeneid*, Book VI, the Elysian fields are contrasted with the "convex" outer surfaces of the earth ("supera ut convexa revisant"), where the spirits of men must reassume bodily form. Because Virgil's Elysium is located *below* the surface of the earth, rather than above it, he employs the adjective *supera*. Despite this difference, however, there is a partial analogy with the contrast that Boccaccio and Chaucer draw between the hero's celestial Elysium and the convexes of the elements he has left behind. The fact that Virgil's Elysium is situated *aeris in campis latis*, "in wide fields of air," made it easier for commentators to interpret his subterranean Elysium in terms of the lunar Elysium of the theologians; see notes 31 through 35 below.

[31] Papias, *s.v. Elysii*: "Elysii campi apud inferos sunt: ubi piorum animae post corporis: animaeque discretionem habitant dicta ἀπὸ τῆς λύσεως idest solutione inter animam & corpus: quod secundum poetas in medio est inferorum suis felicitatibus plenum: Secundum philosophos insulae fortunatae. Secundum theologos iuxta lunarem circulum: ubi iam purior est aer." For other etymological interpretations of Elysium, see Rohde, *Psyche*, I, 82; cf. Rohde's discussion of the locality and inhabitants of Elysium in I, 59, 68, 74-76; II, 561, 571, 574. For classical, medieval, and Renaissance conceptions of Elysium and paradise, see A. Bartlett Giamatti, *The Earthly Paradise and the Renaissance Epic* (Princeton, 1969).

[32] *Servii Grammatici qui feruntur in Vergilii carmina commentarii*, ed. Georgius Thilo et Hermannus Hagen (Hildesheim, 1961), I, 644-645.

Lucanus [IX, 10] *non illuc auro positi, nec ture sepulti perveniunt*.

In his glosses on Book VI, Servius again quotes Lucan as support for the identification of Elysium with the lunar circle (line 640):[33]

largior hic campos aether non nostro largior, sed quam est in cetera inferorum parte. aut re vera largior, si lunarem intelligis circulum: nam, ut supra [V, 735] diximus, campi Elysii aut apud inferos sunt, aut in insulis fortunatis, aut in lunari circulo: Lucanus [IX, 11] *illic postquam se lumine vero induit*.

Subsequently, he explains Virgil's allusion to "airy fields" (line 887) in similar terms: "*aeris in campis* conlisionem fecit. locutus autem est secundum eos, qui putant Elysium lunarem esse circulum."[34]

As Servius interprets Virgil's Elysium, it not only effects the purgation of souls[35]

aliae panduntur inanes suspensa ad ventos [line 741] loquitur quidem poetice de purgatione animorum. . . .

but is also closely associated with the god Mercury, as the conductor of souls after death and as a symbol of reason (line 749):[36]

Deus evocat. . . sed alii Mercurium volunt propter hoc [IV, 242] *hac animas ille evocat orco pallentes, alias sub Tartara tristia mittit*. Et est ratio: nam νοῦς dicitur. . . .

In commenting on the flight of Pompey's soul, several expositors specifically affirm that he has ascended to Elysium and that this is located in the lunar circle. Some of them compare this passage with Virgil's description of Elysium, and many of them suggest that, like other Elysian shades, Pompey's *manes* is undergoing purification in these higher and purer regions of the air. According to the *Adnotationes super Lucanum*, Lucan and Virgil designate the same region between earth and lunar orbit as the abode of the noble dead:

TERRAS INTER LUNAEQUE sapientes ita volunt: spatium, quod

---

[33] *Ibid.*, II, 89.
[34] *Ibid.*, II, 122.
[35] *Ibid.*, II, 104.
[36] *Ibid.*, II, 106.

inter terram et caelum est, possidere animas nobilium defunctorum, inde verum de Anchisa 'aeris in campis latis.'

The same gloss explains that below the lunar circle the air is turbid: "AXIBUS AER hunc dicit, qui vicinus est terris. cum usque ad lunarem circulum turbidus est aer." In this passage (the expositor maintains), Lucan has portrayed the apotheosis of his hero: "BUSTO vult hic ἀποθέωσιν facere poeta Pompeio."[37]

After observing that Lucan's lines describe Pompey's apotheosis ("apotheosis Pompeiana"), the *Commenta Bernensia*[38] contrasts Epicurean, Stoic, and Pythagorean opinions concerning the destiny of the soul with the doctrines of the Peripatetics and Academics, who believe that souls "liberatas a vinculo corporis" return to heaven. In placing the heroes beneath the lunar circle, where the dark air of the sublunary regions meets the inflamed air (i.e., ether) above, the poet has combined Platonic and Stoic doctrines: for the Stoics believed that heroic souls wandered through the air until they were finally dissolved, whereas the Platonists denied a final dissolution:

QUOQ. PATET TERRAS INTER LUNAEQ. MEATUS mixtum dogma cum Platonico Stoicum qui virorum fortium animas existimant in modum siderum vagari in aere et esse sic inmortales, ut non moriantur sed resolvantur secundum Platonem ne resolvantur quidem. quas "semideos manes" dixit, quoniam Graece ἥρωες ἡμίθεοι vocantur id est semidei.

The words *ignea virtus* refer to virtue of soul rather than of body, for the Stoics regarded the soul as fire and Virgil (*Aeneid* VI, 730) spoke of its fiery vigor and celestial origin. In the air beneath the moon, departed souls are purified of contagion before returning to their seats in sun and moon or in the stars:

ET AETERNOS ANIMAM COLLEGIT INORBES animas philosophi tradunt divino igne constare. quae cum sortitae fuerint secundum suum meritum corpus atque eo pollutae contagionem labemque pertulerint, quo etiam dissolutae non carent . . . hoc est aliae ventis per aerem traducuntur, ut purgatae aeris tractu in naturam suam reverti possint.

---

[37] Johannes Endt, ed., *Adnotationes super Lucanum* (Lipsiae, 1909), p. 339.
[38] *Commenta Bernensia*, pp. 289-291.

According to Arnulf of Orleans,[39] the souls that possess the higher virtues return immediately to their proper stars whereas the souls of political leaders must undergo a period of purgation in the air:

Sed ille anime que possident purgatorias vel purgati animi virtutes non morantur in purgatione post dissolutionem corporis, sed statim ad comparem redeunt stellam. Rectoris vero urbium, sicut Pompeii et aliorum anime, purgantur in ipso aere et sicut descendendo aliquid divinitatis in singulis planetis amiserat et corpoream receperat naturam, ita ascendendo exuit ista et recipit priora.

Lucan's "dark air" denotes the region subject to clouds and rains ("aer quantum nubes et pluvie possunt ascendere"). It lies below the moon, but beyond it all things are pure. In this dark air dwell the souls of political virtues until they have been purified and can reascend to their own stars: "In aere nigro sunt anime politicarum virtutum per moram temporis donec ibi purgate ad comparem stellam ascendant. . . . Axes vocat circulos planetarum quorum primus, scilicet luna, a nigro incipit aere. . . . Nec mirum si purgatur ibi Pompeius nam ille locus est in quo prius purgantur sancti viri, et hoc est quod dicit et illud quod patet."

Heroes who dwell in the space between the earth and the moon are called demigods (*semidei*) "non quantum ad genus sed quia eorum conversatio tota est in celis. . . ." Though spirits possessing exemplary virtues can dwell in the higher ether, those endowed with political virtues must dwell in the lowest ether, which is not yet fiery:

Innocuos ignea virtus fecit pacientes etheris quia similibus gaudent similia et se adinvicem pati possunt; si exemplarias haberent virtutes superiorem paterentur etherem, ut angeli, sed quia politicas habebant, ideo in imo erant ethere qui non est adeo igneus.

The commentary in the Biblioteca Medicea-Laurenziana[40] similarly declares that in this region between the earth and the moon, the heroes are purged of the earthly contagion ("ibi purgetur quidquid terrenae fecis") they have contracted.

---

[39] Marti, *Arnulfi . . . glosule*, pp. 431-433.
[40] Codex Laur. Plut. 35. 23, c. 77v.

3

Renaissance commentators similarly interpreted Lucan's lines as a reference to Elysium. According to Sulpizio of Veroli,[41] Pompey's soul has soared to the Elysian fields under the moon, despising the earth and human misery:

pom. animam quae terra condi non potuit in campos elysios qui sub lunae regione sunt evolasse & contemptis terris atque humana miseria in bruti catonisque pectoribus requievisse inquit.

Lucan's *semidei* (Sulpizio suggests) are blessed souls in the lunar circle, and his term *ignea virtus* reflects Platonic and Virgilian beliefs concerning the fiery nature of the soul and the gods. The word *patientes* refers to the purification of the souls in this region, and the phrase *in orbes* alludes to the doctrine that the soul originates in the highest heaven, sinks to earth through the seven spheres, and reascends by the same route.

For Ognibuono[42] this passage describes Pompey's apotheosis and his return *ad comparem stellam*. First, however, he must pass through the region of the heroes, who dwell in the air below the moon and derive their name from this region: "nam luna inferior est planetarum omnium apud quam inferiorem aeris regionem semidei habitant. quos graeci heroas vocant: [lacuna] idest coelo habeantur. *Ignea virtus* reflects the doctrine of the Platonists, "qui animam dicebant esse ignem & deum ipsum . . . sensibilem ignem esse diffinierunt." The term *aetheris imi* distinguishes the region of the heroes from the fiery ether of the heavens, to which the soul is not yet able to ascend:

. . . inferioris respectu caelestis. nam ignis aethereus est omnibus superior elementis: nunc autem dicit non posse quidem animam ad summam aetherem ascendere: sed in medio terrarum ac lunae suum domicilium habere.

After purification in this lower region of the skies, Pompey's spirit will return to its own star, mounting successively through the planetary regions and collecting from each planet the virtues it had lost during its descent:

[41] *Lucanus cum duobus commentis.*
[42] *Ibid.*

Collegit: ideo dixit quia quas virtutes amiserat dum per planetas vel planetarum regiones descendit: eas nunc recuperando colligit in unum sic enim platonici dicebant per planetas animas descendere & ab his virtutem quandam contrahere: ut a saturno pigritiam: a marte iracundiam a Venere libidinem. & sic de caeteris. de quibus vide macrobium.

Non illic auro positi: ad comparem stellam inquit redeunt umbrae tantummodo eorum: qui cum virtute vixerunt: non autem divites sepulchro decorati. secundum platonicos . . . plato & platonici dicebant fortunas [i.e., formas?] esse extra materiam in corporibus caelestibus separatis quorum qualitas sub quaque stella nasceretur: corporibus deinde imprimi ab intrinseco datore videlicet deo. qui formarum dator esse dicitur. & cum e corpore ad stellam comparem redirent sub qua nati sunt.

As both the fixed stars and the air below the lunar concave were commonly regarded as habitations of the blessed, it is not altogether surprising that Ognibuono has apparently placed Pompey in both regions for his backward glance of contempt at the earth and his mortal remains:

primum igitur: [lacuna] idest deificationem loquitur pom. quomodo anima eius ad comparem stellam redierit & deificata sui corporis ludibria contempserit: . . . Postquam se: nunc dicit quomodo pompeius postquam ad regionem illam ubi heroes habitant pervenit loca illa circunspicere coepit. & admiratione quadam perfuxus: respexit ad terras: & locum ubi quasi ludibrium quodam [quoddam?] corpus suum iacebat.

Both Ascensius and Beroaldo explicitly declare that Pompey has ascended to the Elysian fields. According to Beroaldo,[43] "dicit Luca[nus] animam Pompeij petijsse sedes beatorum quae circa lunarem dicuntur esse circulum, & Elysij campi existimantur

---

[43] *Pharsalia* (1514), fol. ccxv. Cf. Beroaldo's commentary on Cicero's dialogue "De contemnenda morte," *M.T. Ciceronis Tuscularum Quaestionum Libri V* (Parisiis, 1549, HEH # 378703), vols. 52-53: "Aliae animae lunarem circulum, aliae solstitialem retinere dicuntur, prout minus magisve purgatae fuerint. Semidei manes habitant, ut autumat Luca[nus] id spatium quod patet inter terras lunae[que] meatus quos virtus ignea fecit imi aetheris patientes. Theologi dixerunt elysium esse circa lunarem circulum, ubi aër purior est: tanquam illuc animi nexibus corporeis solute subvolent. Non me praeterit à quibusdam philosophis elysios campos collocari in sphaera ἀπλανεῖ hoc est inerrabili."

secundum theologos." Here the air is pure, calm, and transparent, in contrast to the "dark" air nearer the earth, which is ruffled by clouds and winds: "Aer que est prope terram ad .xl. stadiorum altitudinem niger est: & in eo nubila ac venti nubesque proveniunt." The souls of heroes and demigods inhabit the higher regions of the air below the fiery ether: "Animae heroum & semideorum aerem habitant & loca quae media sunt inter circulum lunae & terras . . . animae heroum incolunt elementum aeris per cuncta meabilis: quod elemento ignito & aethereo quod summum est, connectit: & sic animae accedunt propius ad aethera inferiorem." The phrase *collegit in orbes* refers to the popular belief recorded by Pliny: "sydera singula singulis esse attributa mortalibus."

According to Ascensius,[44] Lucan has described how "anima Pompeij quae angusto busto contineri nequivit Elysios petiverit. . . ." For the dwelling place of the heroes Ascensius cites two slightly divergent interpretations of Lucan's verses: According to one reading, favored by many scholars, the heroes and demigods dwell *above* the space between the lunar circle and the earth. An alternative reading, however, would place them *within* this space: "Quaque .i. & qua parte, aer patet .i. effunditur inter terras & meatus lunae .i. lunarem circulum, manes semidei .i. spiritus heroum & divorum eorumque qui immortalitatem consecuti sunt per virtutem, habitant .s. post mortem quos .s. manes, virtus ignea .i. coelestis aut divina, fecit existentes innocuos vita, patientes .i. compotes [*sic*] ac tolerativos imi aetheris .i. lunaris globi: ubi mali durare nequeant: & virtus collegit animam Pompeij in aeternos orbes .i. in sphaeras caelestium corporum."

For the majority of these commentators, Pompey's soul has reached the abode of the heroes in the lunar concave. This (many of them explain) is Elysium, and here his *manes* must be purified before it can ascend through the higher regions of fiery ether and return to its own star. As thus conceived, Elysium becomes virtually a pagan purgatory—a Stoic and Neoplatonic staging area between Earth and Heaven. In this classical doctrine of a period of purification after death, which would cleanse the soul of the

---

[44] *Pharsalia* (1514), fol. ccxv.

contagion of earthly sins and inure it to withstand the pure flames of heaven, a medieval Christian might be reminded of the eschatological doctrines of his own faith. (Ascensius hailed one of Lucan's lines as "sententia vel divo Paulo digna"!) For a medieval poet writing on a classical theme, it might provide an expedient means of reconciling the pagan eschatology his subject demanded with the beliefs of his Christian audience.

4

In the tenth book of the *Teseida*[45] the dying Arcita resolves to offer sacrifices to Mercury, beseeching the guide of the dead to conduct his soul to some pleasant place:

> . . . io vorrei a Mercurio litare,
> acciò che esso, per si fatto merto,
> in luogo amen li piaccia di portare
> lo spirito mio, poi che li fia offerto;

After the altar has been kindled, incense burned and offerings made, and the priests have chanted their verses "con voce . . . transmutato," he summons the strength to address six stanzas of petition to Mercury as son of Proserpina, queen of the dead. As before, the emphasis falls on Hermes's role as Psychopompos, the guide who will conduct his soul to appropriate lodgings:

> a cui sta via l'anime portare
> de' corpi, e quelle secondo 'l consiglio
> che da te prendi le puoi allogare. . . .

In particular, Arcita begs to be placed in Elysium, among pious souls: "intra l'anime pie le quai sono in Elisso. . . ." His deeds do not deserve punishment in Hades ("dell'aüra morte degno") as did those of his ancestors, who had justly incurred Juno's ire. He has not committed the crimes of Cadmus or Creon or Oedipus or Semele or Agave. His only offense was to bear arms against Palemone, but for this he can plead Palemone's own example and the excuse of love: "perch'era, sì com'io, innamorato." As his works merit neither Hell nor Heaven, may the god place him in Elysium!:

---

[45] Boccaccio, *Teseida. Delle Nozze d'Emilia*, ed. Aurelio Roncaglia (Bari, 1941), pp. 309-311.

"Dunque tra' neri spiriti non deggio,
o pio iddio, ciò credo, dimorare,
e del ciel non son degno, e i' nol cheggio:
e m'è sol caro in Elisso di stare;
di ciò ti priego e di ciò ti richeggio,
se esser può che tu mel deggi fare;
so che 'l farai, se così se' pio
come suogli esser, venerando iddio."

Shortly thereafter, in the faith the Mercury will answer his prayer, Arcita expires—with Emilia's name on his lips—and begins his flight to the "cielo ottava," whence he follows his guide "nel loco che Mercurio li sortio." If the eighth sphere is indeed the lunar concave, then his prayer has been fully and literally answered; he is in Elysium. This is the end his petition to Mercury has led him (and the reader) to anticipate; it is also (as we have seen) the most probable inference from the opening lines of the second flight stanza.

There remain, however, three further possibilities. If one identifies the *cielo ottava* with the fixed stars (or with any other sphere beyond the moon), then one must conclude either that Boccaccio regards Elysium as located in the *aplanes* (a view recorded by Beroaldo) or else that Mercury has rewarded Arcita far beyond his own hopes or the expectations of the reader. If one accepts the latter view, Boccaccio would appear to have consciously misled his audience, enhancing the element of joyful surprise by bestowing on the hero a higher station than he had looked for, mitigating the tragedy of Arcita's death by a greater felicity than he (or the reader) had anticipated. In this case, the references to Elysium in Arcita's prayer would seem to be a deliberate ruse on the author's part, a false scent to put the reader on the wrong trail and thus heighten the effectiveness of the surprise ending.

Finally, there remains the possibility that Boccaccio may have deliberately exploited the ambiguity of *cielo ottava*, first raising the question of the hero's destination in the prayer stanzas and subsequently leaving the resolution of this problem literally "in the air." By exploiting an equivocal astronomical term the poet might arouse and sustain suspense on questions that might naturally present themselves to the reader: What *does* happen to the souls of pagan heroes? Does a chivalric lover merit the highest sphere or the lowest in the heavens?

Of these four alternatives, the first seems, on the whole, the most plausible. Not only does it complement the Elysium allusions in Arcita's prayer, but it places him in a classical region of purification comparable to the Christian purgatory. In this way Boccaccio preserves the pagan decorum his story demands without violently contradicting the eschatological expectations of his audience.

In transferring the flight stanzas from the story of Arcita to that of Troilus, Chaucer could hardly avoid sacrificing their thematic links with the prayer stanzas. In Arcita's petition that Mercury should guide him to Elysium, Boccaccio had laid the foundation both for the *cielo ottava* to which the hero's soul ascends and for Mercury's role in the apotheosis scene. When Chaucer detached the flight passage from its original context, he inevitably broke the links between this episode and the prayer stanzas, but was nevertheless able to establish other thematic links in their stead. An allusion to Mercury's role as conductor of the dead already existed in the text of the poem, in Troilus's complaint to Pandarus (Book V, lines 321-322):

> "And, god Mercurye, of me now, woful wrecche,
> The soule gyde, and, whan the list, it fecche!"

Unlike Arcita, however, Troilus does not pray for Elysium, though he does in fact inherit it. Ironically, it is Criseyde who expresses the faith that she and her lover will be together in this region (Book IV, lines 788-791):

> For though in erthe ytwynned be we tweyne,
> Yit in the feld of pite, out of peyne,
> That hight Elisos, shal we be yfeere,
> As Orpheus with Erudice his fere."

Ovid's *arva piorum*, where Orpheus rejoined Eurydice,[46] were

---

[46] For allegorical interpretations of Eurydice by Bernard Silvestris, William of Conches, and Nicholas Trivet, see D. W. Robertson, Jr., *A Preface to Chaucer: Studies in Medieval Perspectives* (Princeton, 1962), p. 107n.

located in the underworld (as was Virgil's Elysium), and in Root's opinion[47] this phrase is the probable source of her "feld of pite." Criseyde's allusion to the myth of Orpheus and Eurydice, and the fact that her reference to Elysium apparently replaces an earlier allusion to Pluto's kingdom, suggest that she may possibly have in mind a subterranean region[48]—the Elysium *apud inferos* described by the poets. Like Pompey and Arcita before him, however, Troilus apparently ascends to the Elysium *secundum theologos*—the Elysium *circa lunarem circulum*.

Criseyde's hope to "be yfeere" with her paramour in the Elysian fields—those *campi misericordiae*—remains unfulfilled.[49] Troilus himself does indeed mount to this region, but there is little likelihood that Criseyde will ever join him there.

---

[47] Cf. Robert Kilburn Root, *The Book of Troilus and Criseyde* (Princeton, 1926), p. 514; Ovid, *Metamorphoses*, Book XI, lines 61-66. Bernard L. Witlieb, "Chaucer's Elysian Fields (*Troilus* IV, 789 f.)," *Notes and Queries*, n.s., XVI (1969), 250-251, suggests the *Ovide Moralisé* as the "probable source" of this passage and of Chaucer's description of Elysium as *feld of pite*. Paul M. Clogan, "Chaucer and the *Thebaid* Scholia," *SP*, LXI (1964), 609 f., cites one of Lactantius's glosses on Statius's *Thebaid*, "Elisii campi . . . extra lesionem." As Witlieb observes, Robinson, Tatlock, and Theodore Spencer regard Chaucer's description as reminiscent of Dante's Limbo (*Inferno*, Canto IV, lines 26, 28, 42). J. S. P. Tatlock, "Notes on Chaucer: Earlier or Minor Poems," *MLN*, XXIX (1914), 97; Theodore Spencer, "Chaucer's Hell, A Study in Mediaeval Convention," *Speculum*, II (1927), 182.

[48] Since Pluto's kingdom was sometimes regarded as extending not only over the underworld but also over the *manes* in the atmosphere, Criseyde's allusion does not *necessarily* point to a subterranean location.

[49] Chaucer's phrase *feld of pite* recalls the *campi misericordie* of Arnulf's commentary on the *Pharsalia*. In his gloss on Lucan's line *Sedibus Elysiis campoque expulsa piorum* (Book III, line 12), Arnulf derives the term "Elysian" from *eleison* and refers explicitly to *campi misericordie* (Marti, *Arnulfi . . . glosule*, p. 156):

ELISIIS Eleison id est miserere, inde Elisii campi, quasi campi misericordie ubi requiescebant pii, vel ELISII extra lesionem positi.

Cf. Root's suggestion (p. 514) that Chaucer may have "run across some etymology that connected *Elysium* with Greek ἐλεέω, to have pity . . ."; and my note on this passage in *Notes and Queries*, n.s., XVII (1970), 470 ("Replies").

CHAPTER III

CHAUCER'S FLIGHT ANALOGUES: NARRATIVE CONTEXTS

Having tracked their voyagers (as at some medieval Woomera or Jodrell Bank) to the edge of the moon, Chaucer and Boccaccio abruptly abandon them there. The rest is silence, for there is no indication of a further ascent. Presumably Arcita and Troilus are in Elysium where, as in some fashionable sanatarium, they will profit from the change of air and perhaps from a regimen of purgation. Eventually, they may reascend to their own stars, as Pompey perhaps had done.

On these issues, however, neither poet commits himself, and there is little profit in raising questions that they have tactfully left in darkness. More important are the contexts of these flight episodes, their relationship to the events that immediately precede or follow them, and their bearing on themes expressed elsewhere in the narrative. Thus far we have explored two aspects of these contextual relationships: the role of Mercury as guide of souls and the pagan hope for a *locus amoenus* after death, a tranquil existence in the Elysian fields. We have also noted the literary expediency of both motifs; they enabled the poet to portray the fate of his hero after death through classical conventions, preserving the pagan decorum his characters and setting demanded, without imposing an unnecessary strain on his audience's faith by contradicting Christian eschatological doctrine. The Elysium of Lucan and Virgil and their commentators bore a plausible resemblance to Purgatory; insofar as the flight sequences of Chaucer and Boccaccio reflected this tradition, they acquired a dual authority, both classical and Christian. From these minor but significant links between the flight episodes themselves and mythological motifs introduced earlier in both poems, let us turn to narrative context and ethical themes. Among the flight passages usually regarded as analogues to the *Teseida* and the

Troilus there are significant divergences not only in narrative context but in the very nature of the flight itself.

1

Perhaps the most notable feature of these flight sequences is their tendency to fall into two related but contrasting groups. In several respects, Chaucer and Boccaccio stand much closer to Lucan than to Cicero and Dante. In genre, situation, and other respects, their ascent passages show greater affinities with each other than with either of the other analogues.

In the first place, (allowing for the differences between classical, medieval, and modern definitions of these terms) the *Pharsalia*, the *Teseida*, and the *Troilus* are heroic poetry— "tragedies" belonging to essentially the same genre as Virgil's "high tragedy," the *Aeneid*. Though many Renaissance critics were as acutely conscious as Professor Ker (and other modern scholars) of the differences between epic and romance—though we ourselves can readily perceive the profound gulf that separates Chaucer's "tragedye" from Virgil's *alta tragedia*—we would hardly be justified in imposing our own critical concepts and theoretical distinctions retroactively on the Middle Ages. When Chaucer bids his book to kiss the steps wherein Virgil, Ovid, Homer, Lucan, and Statius have trod, he is paying his homage to epic poets of antiquity; most of them were classical precursors in the same heroic tradition, the same "tragic" genre to which he, as a modern, is also laying claim. (The fact that a modern would probably exclude Ovid from this catalogue and classify both the *Teseida* and the *Troilus* as romances may be of tangential significance, if not an anachronism.) Though Chaucer treats Troilus's loves rather than his warfare and Boccaccio devotes the *Teseida* to wars and loves alike, the context of both poems is the heroic age of Thebes and Troy, and the protagonists move among the most celebrated heroes of classical epic and myth.

Both the *Teseida* and *Troilus* were ambitious undertakings, exhibition pieces conceived on a grand scale and (though a Renaissance neoclassicist might cavil at this judgment) in large part executed in the grand manner. Indeed, their concern for the *stilus grandis* appears to be partly responsible for some of the principal differences modern critics have noted between the *Teseida* and the Knight's Tale and between the *Filostrato* and the *Troilus*.[1] Though I do not intend to reopen the question of what Chaucer actually "did" to either work, it should be noted that the *Teseida* and the *Troilus* seem to show a greater degree of conscious elevation of style than either of the other poems. In reworking Boccaccio's romances, Chaucer appears to have deliberately lowered the style of the one and heightened that of the other. This concern for elevation and gravity in thought and in style[2] is apparent not only in the rhetoric of the *Troilus* and its exploitation of epic conventions, but also in the insertion of Boethian materials. [3]

[1] On Chaucer's relation to Boccaccio's *Filostrato* and *Teseida*, see C.S. Lewis, "What Chaucer Really Did to *Il Filostrato*," *Essays and Studies by Members of the English Association,* XVII (1932), 56-75; *The Filostrato of Giovanni Boccaccio*, trans. Nathaniel Edward Griffin and Arthur Beckwith Myrick (Philadelphia, 1929), pp. 95-107; Robert Kilburn Root, ed., *The Book of Troilus and Criseyde* (Princeton, 1926), pp. xxvi-xl; R. A. Pratt, "Chaucer's Use of the *Teseida*," *PMLA*, LXII (1947), 608-613; Hubertis M. Cummings, *The Indebtedness of Chaucer's Works to the Italian Works of Boccaccio, University of Cincinnati Studies*, X, Part 2 (1916); Hertha Korten, *Chaucers literarische Beziehungen zu Boccaccio* (Hinstorff, 1920); P. M. Kean, "Chaucer's Dealing with a Stanza of *Il Filostrato* and the Epilogue of *Troilus and Criseyde*," *Medium AEvum*, XXXIII (1964), 36-46; Ian C. Walker, "Chaucer and *Il Filostrato*" *English Studies*, XLIX (1968), 318-326.

[2] Cf. Daniel C. Boughner, "Elements of Epic Grandeur in the *Troilus*," *ELH*, VI (1939), 200-210; Bertram Joseph, "*Troilus and Criseyde*: 'A Most Admirable and Inimitable Epicke Poem,' " *Essays and Studies by Members of the English Association*, VII (1954), 42-61; Samuel Marion Tucker, "Chaucer's *Troilus and Criseyde* as an Epos," (Master's thesis,) Columbia University, 1901; Karl Young, "Chaucer's *Troilus and Criseyde* as Romance," *PMLA*, LIII (1938), 38-63.

[3] For Chaucer's debt to Boethius, see Bernard L. Jefferson, *Chaucer and the Consolation of Philosophy of Boethius* (Princeton, 1917); Howard R. Patch, *The Tradition of Boethius: A Study of his Importance in Medieval Culture* (Oxford, 1935); Barnet Kottler, "Chaucer's Boece and the Late Medieval Textual Tradition of the *Consolatio Philosophiae*," (Ph.D. diss., Yale Uni-

The flight stanzas represent yet another device for achieving and maintaining heroic or "tragic" elevation. Associated with classical panegyric (and through Lucan, Virgil, and possibly Ovid with classical epic), the apotheosis of the hero, and his translation to the Elysian fields or to the higher heavens, served the greater glory of Chaucer's Troilus and Boccaccio's Arcita alike. In both instances it enhanced heroic decorum. Having lived and died heroically, both protagonists merit an heroic apotheosis.

The *Commedia*, moreover, is not a heroic poem in the traditional sense of the word (though several Renaissance critics and not a few moderns have regarded it as such), and Dante himself expressly distinguishes its genre from that of Virgil's "high tragedy." It does not derive its subject from the matter of Troy or Thebes or Rome, nor is its protagonist a hero of the conventional martial type. Cicero's protagonist, however, *does* belong to the martial category, and (as Boccaccio undoubtedly realized) both Silius Italicus and Petrarch had written epics in his ancestor's

versity, 1953); John L. Lowes, "Chaucer's Boethius and Jean de Meun," *Romanic Review*, VIII (1917), 383-400; James M. Cline, "Chaucer and Jean de Meun: *De Consolatione Philosophiae*," *ELH*, III (1936), 170-181; V. L. Dedeck-Héry, "Jean de Meun et Chaucer, Traducteurs de la Consolation de Boece," *PMLA*, LII (1937), 967-991; Dedeck-Héry, "Le Boece de Chaucer et les Manuscrits Français de la Consolatio de Jean de Meun," *PMLA*, LIX (1944), 18-25; Kate O. Petersen, "Chaucer and Trivet," *PMLA*, XVIII (1903), 173-193; M. H. Liddell, *Academy*, XLVIII (Sept. 21, 1895), 227; Liddell, *Nation* (New York), LXIV (Feb. 18, 1897), 124 ff.; Patch, "Troilus on Determinism," *Speculum*, VI, 225-243; Charles A. Owen Jr., "The Significance of Chaucer's Revisions of *Troilus and Criseyde*," *MP*, LV (1957-1958), 1-5; John Koch, "Chaucers Boethiusübersetzung," *Anglia*, XLVI (1922), 1-51; John Huber, "Troilus' Predestination Soliloquy: Chaucer's Changes from Boethius," *Neuphilologische Mitteilungen*, LXVI (1965), 120-125; Peter Elbow, "Two Boethian Speeches in *Troilus and Criseyde* and Chaucerian Irony," in *Literary Criticism and Historical Understanding, Selected Papers from the English Institute*, ed. Phillip Damon (New York and London, 1967), pp. 85-107; Theodore A. Stroud, "Boethius' Influence on Chaucer's *Troilus*," *MP*, XLIX (1951-1952), 1-9. On Boethius in medieval tradition, see Edmund T. Silk, *Seculi Noni Auctoris in Boetii Consolationem Philosophiae Commentarius* (Rome, 1935); Kottler, "The Vulgate Tradition of the *Consolatio Philosophiae* in the Fourteenth Century," *Mediaeval Studies*, XVII (1955), 209-214.

honor. Nevertheless, the *Somnium Scipionis* is not a poem at all; it is a prose dream vision inserted in a philosophical dialogue.

Second, in Lucan, Boccaccio, and Chaucer, the flight is represented as an actual occurrence, rather than as an allegorical journey or a visionary ascent. Even though it is really a poetic invention, it is placed within the context of history and narrated as though it were a historical event. The mode of imitation is not transumptive, but literal. Though the journey includes an act of contemplation, it is more than a mere symbol of contemplation; it is not a purely imaginary ascent, but a real flight to the heavens. As heroic or "tragic" poets, all three writers are also poets "historial," but in different senses, Lucan bases his narrative on historical persons and events, and (though he appears too credulous, too biased, too fond of rhetorical ornament and of the marvelous to merit this title) Renaissance critics accused him of being a historian rather than a poet. Chaucer and Boccaccio rely heavily on legendary materials and on the inventions of their own imaginations, but they nevertheless place their fictions within the historical context of wars traditionally believed to have been real.

Scipio's flight to the heavens, however, is purely imaginary, even though the characters are historical persons; it occurs in a dream vision inserted in a treatise on politics. Dante's ascent occurs in an allegorical vision, though he depicts his ascent as an actual journey. In contrast to the exclusively narrative mode whereby the "tragic" poets describe the ascent, both Dante and Scipio rely on a mixture of narrative and dialogue.

Third, in the three "tragic" poets the flight from earth to heaven constitutes a single episode in a much longer narrative. Cicero devotes the entire *Somnium* to his hero's ascent to the stars and his dialogue with his ancestor. Though Dante's ascent to the sphere of the fixed stars and contemplation of the planets and the world form a single episode in his poem, his passage through the heavens occupies the whole *Paradiso*. Though the *Somnium* and the *Paradiso* are merely parts of larger works, both give central emphasis to the theme of the heavenly felicity of virtuous souls after death, and in both the ascent through the heavens constitutes the basis of the entire action. In the three "tragedies," however, the ascent motif and the theme of heavenly beatitude are relegated to a handful of verses, a brief episode in a long heroic narrative of love or war.

Fourth, in Lucan, Boccaccio, and Chaucer, the astral voyagers are the ghosts of dead heroes, warriors who have fought at Thebes and Troy and in the provinces of the Roman Empire. In Dante and Cicero they are living men, not apotheosized shades. The heroic somnambulist (or "somnivolant") and the contemplative pilgrim in search of the celestial city and of a people just and sane—these are living voyagers on (so to speak) a conducted sight-seeing tour through the mansions of the dead. In both cases the traveler's final apotheosis is still to come; he has still to make the same ascent after death. In contrast to the journeys undertaken by the *manes* of Pompey, Arcita, and Troilus, the pilgrimages of Dante and Scipio do not represent the apotheosis of a departed soul. Instead, they are essentially voyages of exploration, expeditions undertaken for the sake of spiritual, if not scientific, discovery. They are surveys of moral uranography, and Dante's celestial map is scarcely less specific or less detailed than the world maps of the medieval cosmographer.

Though the differences between the two groups of analogues in this respect may seem too obvious to require further discussion, they are nevertheless significant insofar as they have conditioned the relative emphasis placed on eschatological doctrines in all five of these works and the manner in which such doctrines have been presented. Though all five examples depict the felicity of righteous or heroic spirits after death, the three "epic" poets present it primarily in relation to the events of the plot and, in particular, to the death of the hero. In these works the emphasis falls on the hero's personal felicity, his personal merits and rewards, his personal magnanimity, his personal contempt of *terrena* and love of *coelestia*. Whereas Cicero and Dante elaborate the concepts of felicity, merit, and reward—and contempt for the world—into a complex eschatological system, the three "epic" poets treat them more briefly, more simply, and less systematically, placing primary stress on the relationship between the protagonist's celestial reward and the circumstances of his life and death. In none of these three "tragedies" can the flight sequence be detached from the death scene that has preceded it.

Though all these men learn to despise *temporalia* and *terrena*, not all possess the gift of laughter, nor do they direct their mirth at the same objects. Scipio does not laugh at all. Dante laughs (or smiles) at the *vil sembiante* of the tiny earth in comparison with the heavens; unlike Lucan's hero, he is in no position to laugh at his own funeral. The fact that he makes his ascent as a living man has robbed him of at least one potential source of astral merriment. Under the circumstances, only Troilus and Arcita can join Pompey in deriding their own death and the fate of their mortal remains.

In Scott's opinion, the chief evidence for Boccaccio's indebtedness to the *Pharsalia* consists in "the fact that Pompey and Arcita are both, in their celestial station, moved to laughter by the sight of what took place after their death . . . especially if Boccaccio . . . took 'ludibria' to refer to the cremation of Pompey by the mourning Cordus rather than to the mutilation of his body by his enemies."[4] This passage had been (and would be) variously interpreted: as a reference to Pompey's body, to the indignities inflicted on it, and to his sepulcher. According to the *Commenta Bernensia*, Pompey is laughing at his headless body: "RISITQUE SUI LUDIBRIA TRUNCI id est corporis, ut sit sensus: sui corporis trunci."[5] Arnulf maintains that after acquiring true knowledge Pompey regards as a jest the body he had hitherto loved for so long: "et tunc pro ludibrio habuit suum corpus quod tanto tempore prius amavit."[6] The *Adnotationes*, however, identifies the object of his laughter as his sepulcher; having been received into heaven, he ridicules the vanity of a tomb: "TRUNCI vanitatem scilicet sepulchri risit, cum ipse esset receptus in caelum."[7] Early Renaissance commentaries exhibit a compara-

---

[4] Forrest S. Scott, "The Seventh Sphere: A Note on *Troilus and Criseyde*," *MLR*, II (1956), 4n.

[5] *Commenta Bernensia*, p. 292.

[6] Arnulfus, p. 434.

[7] Johannes Endt, ed., *Adnotationes super Lucanum* (Lipsiae, 1909), p. 340.

ble variety. Sulpizio glosses *ludibria* merely as "irrisionem & contemptum."[8] In Ognibuono's opinion, Pompey despises the maltreatment of his body, because his spirit has been apotheosized: "& deificata sui corporis ludibria contempserit." Though his ashes have been confined *in angusto ac sordido sepulchro*, his soul has been elevated *in celestem regionem*, and ridicules the mutilation of his corpse: "Ludibria trunci: cum videret truncum corpus sui: ita dilacerari: primo quidem fluctibus maris: deinde semiustum condi sepulchro quasi risum continere non potuit."[9] Ascensius in turn explains this passage as an allusion to the indignities perpetrated by the Egyptians: "& risit, id est vilipendit & pro nihilo habuit, ludibria .i. irrisionem & contemptum sui trunci .i. quae fecerant Aegyptij in corpus suum. quae corpori propter corpus fiunt, non nocent nec prosunt animae: licet solatia sint vivis."[10]

Various though they are, these interpretations are not mutually exclusive, and it is possible that Boccaccio or Chaucer may have recognized more than one point of resemblance between Pompey's laughter and that of Troilus or Arcita. Though Pompey laughs at his dishonored body or incomplete funeral rites, Arcita at the grief of the hydra-headed crowd, and Troilus at the tears of his survivors, these are not the complete (nor perhaps even the principal) objects of their contempt. The outburst of laughter is merely the culminating episode in an act of contemplation that, beginning with the heavens, turns to the earth and finds it despicable and vile in comparison. In the final analysis, the hero's contempt is directed to the world itself, to the blindness of humanity, and to the vanity of earthly bliss. His laughter merely brings this *contemptus mundi* into focus. Displaying his own magnanimity (his greatness of mind or soul) by deriding the fate of his own body, he can laugh at the vanity of tears and funeral rites. These are doubly vain—not only because the soul is alive but because (in Lucan's phrase) "nec illuc auro positi nec ture

---

[8] *Lucanus cum duobus commentis.*
[9] *Ibid.*
[10] *Pharsalia* (1514), fol. ccxv.

sepulti Perveniunt": neither golden coffins nor burial with incense conducts a man to the heavens, but *ignea virtus* alone. In tranquillity of mind and the knowledge of true felicity, he can afford (like patience on a monument) to smile at grief.

In the opinion of one medieval commentator, Pompey laughed at the "vanity of his tomb," because he himself had been received in heaven. Perhaps this is one of the considerations that moved Arcita and Troilus to deride the grief of their survivors. It may be significant, moreover, that both Chaucer and Boccaccio employ the word *vanity*, though Lucan himself had not used this term. After laughing at the grief of the crowd, Arcita condemns "la vanitate . . . dell' umane genti", and immediately before the laughter scene Troilus has "held al vanite" in comparison with the full felicity of heaven. An alternative suggestion—that Pompey now regards as a jest the body he had hitherto loved—could be even more appropriate for the romantic heroes of the *Teseida* and the *Troilus*, whose lives and deaths have been strongly influenced by the lusts of the flesh. Arcita condemns the blindness of those who "seguon del mondo la falsa biltate, lasciando il cielo"; and Troilus similarly damns "al oure werk that folweth so The blynde lust" instead of seeking heaven.

Nevertheless, though there are (as Scott observed) important analogies between the flight episodes of the *Teseida* and the *Pharsalia*, there are also significant differences, and these seem to place Boccaccio's elaborate account of Arcita's funeral in an ironic light. In pursuing epic and heroic decorum, Boccaccio not only apotheosizes his hero but proceeds, immediately afterward, to endow him with funeral honors equally worthy of a hero. Arcita's pyre is a magnificent affair that contrasts singularly with Pompey's *semusta membra . . . Degeneremque rogum*. If Pompey could find cause for mirth in his "charred limbs and unworthy pyre" or in the vanity of his sepulcher, how would Arcita have reacted to his own *pompa funebre*? The burst of laughter that precedes this scene undercuts its solemnity and undermines its epic dignity. Whether Boccaccio intended this effect, however, is another matter.

In one respect Troilus and Pompey stand apart from the other voyagers. These are the only ones whose bodies have suffered mutilation and other barbarities. Arcita expires surrounded by friends; he does not perish in battle, and he survives his fatal accident long enough to wed Emilia, bid farewell to friends and relatives, and offer sacrifices to propitiate the gods. Pompey's body, on the contrary, is beheaded in the sight of his wife and followers, and cast to the mercy of the waves. Though it is subsequently retrieved by a loyal retainer, there is insufficient fuel for a funeral pyre, and the remains must be inurned *semusta*—"half-burned." Troilus's corpse is likewise subjected to indignities. According to Virgil, he falls from his chariot and is dragged along the ground by his own horses. In medieval accounts, however, Achilles beheads him and drags his body about the city of Troy.[11] Chaucer himself does not mention these details, merely declaring that "ful pitously hym slough the fierse Achille"; but the full "pity" of Troilus's death depends on an awareness of how he met his end. The fate of Pompey and Troilus is far more miserable, more "pitous" than that of Arcita, and their celestial mirth stands proportionately in sharper contrast.

The laughter of Pompey, Troilus, and Arcita, following so shortly after their miserable ends, is reminiscent of the Stoic theme developed by Cicero in his first Tusculan Disputation ("De contemnenda morte") and by Seneca in his various Consolations. After praising Socrates and other Greek worthies for their scorn of death and extolling Theramenes for dying with a jest,[12] Cicero exhorts the wise man to show a similar contempt for the manner of his burial. Though "Achilles fastens Hector to his chariot and drags him," he has "not dragged Hector . . . but the body which had been Hector's." The complaint of Deiphilus's ghost and its plea for burial are (Cicero continues) ridiculous: "I do not understand what he is afraid of, seeing that he pours out such a stream of fine seven-foot verses." Condemning the "deep . . . deception" of those who think "the grave is the body's haven," Cicero passes to the funeral customs of the Egyptians and other

---

[11] Root, *The Book of Troilus*, pp. 470, 559.
[12] Cicero, *Tusculan Disputations*, pp. 115, 122.

superstitious practices, concluding that "this whole subject . . .
must be treated with contempt as regards ourselves, but not
ignored in the case of those connected with us. . . ."[13] Many of
the commonplaces in this passage would recur in Lucan's account
of Pompey's Stoic contempt of death and burial. Some of them
may have been in Boccaccio's mind when he described Arcita's
laughter at the grief of the mob; they would have been even
more relevant for Troilus, who had traditionally suffered a fate
remarkably similar to that of Hector.

Since the apotheosis had become a conventional heroic motif,
and Elysium a conventional reward of heroism, it was fitting that
both Chaucer and Boccaccio should place the ascent of their
martial shades in a heroic context. Arcita dies after a formal
combat in the lists (though his death results from other factors)
and receives the funeral honors of a classical hero. Troilus is slain
after slaying "thousandes" on the battlefield. Near the very end of
the poem, after recounting the unfortunate conclusion of Troilus's
love affair, Chaucer returns to the theme of martial valor, emphasizing the conventional heroic virtues and gests—Troilus's
"knyghthod and his grete myght," his exploits in "cruel bataille,"
his "armes" and "worthi dedes," his "ire" and "wraththe." As the
poet reminds us in the end, Troilus "was withouten any peere,
Save Ector," and his death follows closely upon that of his
brother, who had met so similar a fate at the hands of the "fierse
Achille." Hector himself was traditionally included among the
Nine Worthies, ranking with Alexander and Julius Caesar among
classical heroes; and in the *Nicomachean Ethics* Aristotle had
cited him as an example of *virtus heroica*. As second only to
Hector, Troilus moves in very high company indeed. His final
exploits belong to the traditional decorum of the military hero,
and he receives a characteristically heroic reward.

At this point the celestial voyagers part company. After
soaring to the threshold of heaven, Pompey returns to earth to

---

[13] *Ibid.*, pp. 129, 131.

survey his former battlefield and to inspire a future avenger.[14]

Then his spirit flew above the field of Pharsalia, the standards of bloodthirsty Caesar, and the ships scattered over the sea, till it settled as the avenger of guilt, in the righteous breast of Brutus, and took up its abode in the heart of unconquerable Cato.

Dante continues his ascent through the higher spheres to the Empyrean. Scipio presumably wakes up. Troilus and Arcita follow their celestial chamberlain to the quarters set apart for them.

2

In Pompey's ascent to Elysium, at least one medieval commentator recognized the appropriate reward of political virtue; the *rector urbis* merited an abode among the heroes in the lower ether, but was not yet able to endure the intense flame of the upper heavens. Arcita and Troilus similarly receive a reward conventionally associated with martial heroes. Nevertheless, all three of these flight passages exhibit the influence of an intellectual tradition that had extolled a higher type of virtue and a loftier mode of heroism—the wisdom of the Stoic or Neoplatonic sage. Just as the Neoplatonists had exalted the purgative and exemplary virtues and the virtues of the purified soul above the political virtues, so the Stoics had ranked the wise man above the heroes celebrated in myth and epic song.[15] "In Cato," Seneca believed, "the immortal gods had given to us a truer exemplar of the wise man than earlier ages had in Ulysses and Hercules. For we Stoics have declared that these were unconquered by struggles, were despisers of pleasure, and victors over all terrors. Cato did not grapple with wild beasts.. . . He stood alone against the vices of a degenerate state. . . ."

Subjected to the scrutiny of classical philosophers, the Elysium of the poets acquired new shades of meaning unanticipated by

[14] *Lucan*, trans. J. D. Duff, Loeb Classical Library (London and New York, 1928), p. 505.

[15] Seneca, *Moral Essays*, I, 51, 53; *De Constantia Sapientis*.

Homer, and these, in turn, would leave their imprint on later generations of poets. Once regarded as the exceptional privilege of a few elect spirits, Elysium had become the natural prerogative not only of martial heroes but of contemplative heroes. Like other myths, it had become rationalized in terms of natural as well as moral law. By the laws of physics as well as the rule of justice, the newly liberated soul—now significantly lighter after its separation from the body—would naturally reascend to the heavens in proportion to its freedom from earthly contagion. The speed and altitude of its ascent were conditioned by its purity from worldly affections and carnal appetites.

To the Stoics and Neoplatonists who had debated the subtler points of eschatology, no class of humanity seemed more preeminently worthy of the heavens than the philosopher. Purified by the study of philosophy, the soul of the wise man mounted more rapidly through the skies than the ghosts of lesser men—spirits dragged down by worldly desires and encumbered by the weight of material cares. Only by radically divesting itself of this earthly dross, only through purification, could the soul regain its natural levity and reascend to its native heaven, to its "true country" or *patria*. Its return to the skies depended not merely on divine justice but on natural law; not only on meritorious deeds but on purification from worldly contagion.

If the felicity of blessed souls consisted primarily in contemplation of the heavens, the attainment and continued enjoyment of such felicity depended largely on their liberation from worldly desires. Hence in Stoic or Neoplatonic meditations on death and in the poetry of Lucan and his imitators the two motifs are frequently combined. The theme of admiration of the heavens is coupled with a converse motif, the theme of *contemptus mundi*. As both are associated with Stoic or Neoplatonic pneumatology, both frequently recur together in the poetic apotheoses composed by writers sympathetic to these doctrines. In Lucan's account of Pompey's ascent we encounter, not surprisingly, a cluster of ideas already intimately associated with the Stoic wise man: contemplation of heaven and earth and comparison of the two; admiration of the heavens and contempt of the world; the contrast between heavenly knowledge and earthly ignorance, between true and false felicity, or between permanent and transient glory.

Lucan inherited these *topoi* from classical philosophy, and (though his perfect exemplar of the Stoic *sapiens* was Cato) applied them to Pompey's apotheosis. Enriched by the glosses of medieval commentators, they passed to Dante and Boccaccio and Chaucer.

As a result of this emphasis on "heroic knowledge,"[16] the ascent of the Stoic or Platonic wise man to the heavens came to signify much more than a mere reward for a life devoted to wisdom and virtue. It became an actual means of purifying virtue and perfecting wisdom. It became essentially a contemplative voyage of the intellect. In this way the poetic hero acquired some of the characteristics of the Stoic or Neoplatonic philosopher. He, too, was filled with admiration as he contemplated the movements of the celestial bodies. He, too, felt contempt for the world as he directed his gaze downward (*despexit*) and beheld the relative darkness and minute size of the earth. With its double sense—to look down and to despise—the verb *despicere* lent itself readily to the theme of *contemptus mundi*; and, though neither Lucan nor Boccaccio employs it in this context, Chaucer rings the changes on this concept in his own flight passage, devoting almost an entire stanza to variations on the literal meaning of *despise*: "doun . . . gan avyse," "gan despyse," "held al vanitee," "his loking doun he caste."

In these verses as in Seneca's *To Polybius on Consolation*, one encounters a similar juxtaposition of the motifs of admiration of the heavens and contempt of the world, a contempt that is accentuated by the equivocal verb *despicere*. The analogy is significant not as an argument for Chaucer's possible indebtedness to Seneca's *consolatio*, but as testimony to the continuity of Stoic tradition:[17]

---

[16] See Arnold Stein, *Heroic Knowledge: An Interpretation of Paradise Regained and Samson Agonistes* (Minneapolis, 1957).

[17] Seneca, *Moral Essays*, II, 378-380.

Si est aliquis defunctis sensus, nunc animus fratris mei velut ex diutino carcere emissus, tandem sui iuris et arbitrii, gestit et rerum naturae spectaculo fruitur et humana omnia ex loco superiore despicit, divina vero, quorum rationem tam diu frustra quaesierat, propius intuetur.

Most of these themes are implicit in Lucan's account of Pompey's apotheosis and explicitly developed by medieval or Renaissance commentators. In explaining the rational movement of Pompey's soul, Arnulf declares that following the motion of the firmament means despising earthly things and seeking the Creator alone ("terrena omnino contempnere et in solum Creatorem intendere").[18] Sulpizio similarly refers to Pompey's contempt of the world and human misery: "contemptis terris atque humana miseria."[19]

In Lucan's description of how Pompey "steeped himself in the true light of that region, and . . . saw the thick darkness that veils our day," many commentators detected the contrast between earthly ignorance and heavenly wisdom. Arnulf of Orleans[20] explains *lumine vero* as "sapientia; divina scientia enim illuminat quemlibet dum ignorat cecum existentem. VERO quia 'sapientia huius mundi stulticia est apud Deum.'" Glossing *inplevit* as "habundanter," Arnulf adds that "nichil perfectum in rebus humanis, sed in celestibus summa perfectio." *Sub nocte* means "obscuritate. NOSTRA DIES scilicet humana, vel illud etiam quod a nobis dies vocatur, scilicet nostra scientia. . . ."

Sulpizio[21] similarly explains *vero* as signifying "clarissimo nam hoc nostrum illi collatum est tenebrosum." *Nocte* denotes "tenebris," and *nostra dies* means "lux & vita humana." Ognibuono explains the phrase *implevit lumine vero* as Pompey's return to his own star: "idest reversus est in comparem stellam cuius qualitatem & splendorem concepit." *Nostra dies* refers to the comparative darkness of earthly light in comparison with that of the heavens: "quia ad aereae comparationem lux terrarum

---

[18] Arnulfus, p. 433.
[19] *Lucanus cum duobus commentis.*
[20] Arnulfus, p. 434.
[21] *Lucanus cum duobus commentis.*

tenebrae potius dici debent." Beroaldo[22] glosses *nocte* as "tenebris," citing Lucretius: "Qualibus in tenebris vitae quantisque periclis degitur hoc aevi." Ascensius[23] explains *vero lumine* as "vera cognitione rerum," and earthly night as ignorance: "vidit sub quanta nocte, id est ignoratione rerum iaceret dies nostra, id est nos in hac mortali vita. . . . "

Lucan devotes far less space to his hero's illumination than do his imitators, though the latter could conceivably have encountered a detailed discussion of this point in Arnulf's commentary. Where Pompey contrasts the "true light" of heaven with the darkness of "our day," both Arcita and Troilus specifically contrast the small size of the earth with the grandeur of the skies. On this point they are following a commonplace exploited in Stoic consolations and Neoplatonic treatises, in medieval astronomical manuals, and in Christian religious works. From this comparison Arcita learns to disregard "ogni cosa da nulla stimare a rispetto del ciel. . . ." Troilus's scorn is expressed in stronger terms—full contempt of the world in comparison with the full felicity of heaven:

> . . . and fully gan despise
> This wrecched world, and held al vanite
> To respect of the pleyn felicite
> That is in hevene above: . . .

Where Pompey merely laughs at *sui ludibria trunci*, Arcita extends his scorn to the mortal ignorance that pursues the false beauty of the world instead of seeking the heavens:[24]

> . . . la vanitate
> forte dannando dell' umane genti,
> li quai, da tenebrosa cechitate
> mattamente oscurati nelle menti,
> seguon del mondo la falsa biltate,
> lasciando il cielo; . . .

Though this passage may conceivably echo Lucan's *quanta sub*

---

[22] *Pharsalia* (1514), fol. ccxv.

[23] *Ibid*., fol. ccxv.

[24] Boccaccio, *Teseida. Delle Nozze d'Emilia*, ed. Aurelio Roncaglia (Bare, 1941), p. 316.

nocte (a passage sometimes glossed as *obscuritate* or *tenebris*), the allusion to the world's "false beauty" is Boccaccio's own addition. Chaucer, in turn, retains the allusion to earthly ignorance in the epithet *blynde*, but converts this passage into a condemnation of worldly pleasure as fleeting and impermanent:

> And dampned al oure werk that folweth so
> The blynde lust, the which that may nat laste;
> And sholden al oure herte on heven caste.

3

In all three instances the hero's *contemptus mundi* is couched both in general and in personal terms, referring not only to the universal condition of mankind but to his own individual situation. Logically and rhetorically, moreover, all three flight passages center upon the category of Place; from his particular *locus* in the concave of the eighth sphere, the voyager successively contemplates the entire heavens, the whole earth, and finally —more narrowly—the particular site where his body lies ("al loco là dove aveva il suo corpo lasciato"). In each case the laughter that he directs toward his cadaver (or toward the emotions that others display toward his remains) serves as an index of his newly regained liberty of spirit. For it is only through complete separation both from the body and from bodily lusts that he can regain his native heavens. That he has learned to despise not only his body and the treatment it receives from his survivors but also the needs and desires of the flesh is proof of his magnanimity—his greatness of mind and soul.

Just as Pompey's laughter at *sui ludibria trunci* is closely linked with his personal situation—the circumstances of his death and funeral rites—the condemnation of *blynde lust* and pursuit of the world's *falsa biltate* are equally relevant to the personal experience of Troilus and Arcita. The latter has sought the world's "false beauty"; indeed, shortly before his death, marveling at Emilia's beauty, he has wondered whether he could possibly leave so fair a creature behind.[25] Troilus has blindly placed his

---

[25] *Ibid.*, p. 298; Book X, stanzas 53-56.

trust in worldly pleasure—a felicity that is by nature transitory. In both instances this general condemnation of the follies of mankind is personally motivated; it is not merely a universal judgment but a personal condemnation of the hero's own folly, exposed and reviewed in the light of newly acquired insight. In both cases, moreover, this judgment is closely linked with the amused detachment with which he regards his own body and the attitudes of his survivors toward his corpse. Both of these scenes ultimately derive from Lucan's *sui ludibria trunci*; in both, the *locus* or focal point of the hero's *despectus* is the spectacle of his lifeless corpse and the group of mourners assembled about it. Nevertheless, there is one minor difference. Whereas Boccaccio retains the allusion to *corpo*, Chaucer includes a variation that explicitly links this scene with the reference to Troilus's death and the beginning of the flight sequence. The repetition of the same verb ("slough" and "slayn") in lines 1806, 1807, and 1820 not only heightens the unity of this passage but gives additional emphasis to the obvious, but central, theme in these stanzas: the contrast between the death of the body and the immortality of the soul.

In both flight passages, in the *Troilus* as in the *Teseida*, there is an implicit link between the hero's derision of the body and his condemnation of bodily appetites once passionately indulged and now outgrown. Not only are they juxtaposed within the same stanzaic context, but both represent relatively complex variations on Lucan's simpler theme. Chaucer's censure of *blynde lust* and Boccaccio's strictures on the world's *falsa biltate* both take their point of departure, in the final analysis, from Lucan's *ludibria trunci*.

4

Though Lucan provides a comparatively simple account of Pompey's accession to "heroic knowledge," medieval glosses offered a more detailed account, stressing the motifs of *contemptus mundi*, divine love, and the return to "rational" movements. Both Chaucer and Boccaccio emphasize many of the same themes, and it is conceivable that their variations on the *Pharsalia* may have been influenced by the commentaries. According to Arnulf,[26] Lucan's *ignea virtus* refers to virtue joined with divine love: "IGNEA VIRTUS id est illa que non est sola sed ubi est amor divinus, et multe virtutes isti tali coherent virtuti." The phrase *collegit animam* refers to the movement of the soul's intent from worldly objects to contemplation of the Creator: "COLLEGIT ANIMAM, id est vim anime plenariam quam in corpore parum habebat, exuta a corpore recepit plenarie, quia quedam scit in corpore sed omnia extra corpus, vel COLLEGIT quia prius sparsa in mundanis ad unum quid tunc colligitur, scilicet ad contemplationem Creatoris. ORBES ETERNOS vocat identitatem sue intentionis. Nam in corpore aliquando intendit viciis, aliquando virtutibus, extra corpus soli contemplationi divinorum."

Macrocosm and microcosm alike—the greater universe and the little world of man—are moved by both rational and irrational motions. When, on the one hand, the human soul intends its Creator, it follows a rational movement, corresponding to the motion of the *aplanes* (or *coelum stellatum*) from east to west. When, on the other hand, the soul diverts its intent from the Creator to the creature—from spiritual to secular things—it follows an irrational movement, comparable to the motion of the planets from west to east:

Nota etiam duos motus esse, unum rationalem, alium irrationalem. Applanos ab oriente in occidentem, per occidentem iterum in orientem volvitur qui motus dicitur rationalis, quia ratus et firmus est. Planete volvuntur ab occidente in orientem, per orientem iterum in occidentem qui motus dicitur irrationalis, quia aliquando sunt stationarii secundum visum nostrum, non tamen sunt. Et hii duo motus dicuntur esse in microcosmo, id est in minori mundo, scilicet in anima humana. Quando intendit in Creatorem suum tunc, quamvis per occidentem volvatur, non tamen facit ibi moram; cum autem non immoretur in orientem sed revertitur, tunc irrationaliter currit et facit hominem in secularibus intentum tantummodo. . . . Omnis enim homo necessario rationalem ut irrationalem habet.

The commentary in the Biblioteca Medicea-Laurenziana *Pharsalia* (Laur. Plut. 35.23) interprets Pompey's ascent in terms of

---

[26] Arnulfus, pp. 432-434.

"rational" motion and *contemptus mundi*. Hitherto dispersed among worldly things and given over to the "temporal motion of reason," the soul is now "collected" in the eternal spheres and gathered up in the "eternal motion of reason." Another gloss in the same manuscript interprets Lucan's references to *astra fixa* and *nocte* in similar terms: "& attendens motum rationabilem omnia mundana despexit, nostra dies bene dicitur nox ad illam claritatem."[27]

Though medieval commentators exhibited no little ingenuity in detecting the macrocosm-microcosm ratio and the theory of rational motions in the *Pharsalia*, there is no explicit allusion to this doctrine in the text itself, and one suspects that such an interpretation might move Lucan, like Pompey, to laughter. Although Dante exploits the analogy between the movements of the *aplanes*[28] and the human soul, this motif is no more explicit in the flight stanzas of Boccaccio and Chaucer than in Lucan's own lines. If the commentaries influenced either author on this point, the influence would seem to be very general indeed, appearing in the hero's return from secular to celestial concerns, from irrational to rational intention, and from earthly affections to divine love. Though both passages *do* portray a final return to reason, this is expressed not through the macrocosm-microcosm ratio, but through the juxtaposition of Stoic commonplaces whose close association we have noted earlier: admiration of the heavens and contempt of the world.

Finally, the hero's return to reason, from irrational to rational motion,[29] may have been figuratively expressed in the role of

[27] Codex Laur. Plut. 35.23, c. 77v.

[28] See Lewis and Short, *A Latin Dictionary* (Oxford, 1907), *s.v. aplanes*; Liddell and Scott, *A Greek-English Lexicon* (Oxford, 1925), *s.v.* ἀπλανής. For the variant *aplanos*, see R. E. Latham, *Revised Mediaeval Latin Word-List from British and Irish Sources* (London, 1965), *s.v. aplanos*.

[29] Nicholas Trivet draws an analogy between the rational and irrational movements of the heavens and the motions of flesh and spirit within the human soul in his commentary on Boethius's *De Consolatione* (Book I, prose 4). The "vita humana rationalis" resembles the order ("ordinis") of the

Mercury In commenting on Virgil's Elysium and Mercury's office as guide of souls, Servius had identified the god with *ratio* or *nous*. This interpretation was conventional,[30] and if Boccaccio and Chaucer recalled it, it would have heightened the element of "heroic knowledge" in their flight episodes. After contemplating the heavens and the earth—after acquiring knowledge of true and false *biltate* or true and false felicity—Arcita and Troilus are conducted to their stations in the heavens by Reason itself.

5

Though all five of these flight sequences belong to a common tradition and share many of its conventional motifs, most of them are parts of larger works that vary widely in genre and subject matter, in structure and style, in character and plot. (The *Somnium Scipionis* is only a partial exception; an episode in Cicero's lost dialogue *De Republica*, it survived independently of its original matrix, thanks to the popularity of Macrobius's commentary.) Comparisons between the flight scenes themselves are likely to be misleading unless the critic takes into consideration the similarities and differences between the larger wholes to which these scenes belong.

---

heavens; "sicut motus erraticus planetarum retorquatur rationabili motu firmamenti. ita erraticus motus carnis a rationabili spiritu dicitur refrenari." In the order and harmony of the erratic stars, their irrational movements subordinated to the rational motion of the firmament, Troilus and Arcita might behold an image of the subordination of passion to reason and flesh to spirit within the human soul. See HEH MS EL9H9, fol. 115 ("Incipit commentum fratris Nicholai Tryvet super quinque libros Boecii de consolatione philosophie"). For permission to quote from this manuscript, I am indebted to the Curator of Manuscripts and the Librarian of the Henry E. Huntington Library. Except where otherwise specified, all references to Trivet's commentary in this study are based on this manuscript. For additional references to rational and irrational movements of the heavens in medieval literature and for recent studies of this tradition in Dante and Donne, see Chauncey Wood, *Chaucer and the Country of the Stars: Poetic Uses of Astrological Imagery* (Princeton, 1970), pp. 231n-234n.

[30] In his commentary on Book IV, meter 3, of the *Consolation*, Trivet describes Mercury as "deus prudencie" (fol. 166).

Since the function of these episodes has been strongly conditioned by their narrative or dialectical context, they sometimes exhibit marked variations even when they are developing similar themes. Though all these scenes stress the "heroic knowledge" of the liberated soul, admiration of the heavens, and contempt of the world, they do not always select the same values for emphasis. Though the sharp distinction between temporal and eternal goods is common to them all, they stress different facets of this commonplace. Dante exploits this dichotomy to define the respective jurisdictions of emperor and pope. Lucan employs it to contrast the true knowledge that the separated soul acquires in heaven, with its comparative ignorance on earth, where it was subject to the limitations of the body. Cicero utilizes this *topos* to accentuate the difference between perpetual and transient fame. For Boccaccio, it underscores the contrast between true and false beauty; for Chaucer, the opposition between stability and mutability, constant and inconstant felicity.

In their exploitation of the *contemptus mundi* theme these works show similar variations. Pompey laughs at his half-cremated body and the vanity of funeral rites and sepulchers; his own fiery virtue—not the flames of the funeral pyre—has lifted him to the heavens. When Dante smiles at the earth's "vile semblance" and praises those who turn their thoughts to the skies, he has just heard Saint Benedict roundly denounce the contemporary members of his order for neglecting his rule and seeking worldly wealth instead of ascending the ladder of contemplation, a theme that recurs throughout the *Paradiso* and indeed the entire *Commedia*. Scipio learns the vanity of earthly fame; Troilus and Arcita the vanity of worldly love.

All five of these episodes function as rhetorical *exempla*, imparting greater vividness and forcefulness to the writer's general theme by giving it concrete expression in terms of the experience of a particular individual. Utilizing the demonstrative and forensic *topoi* of praise and justice to eulogize human merit or defend the wisdom and equity of divine governance, these authors also exploit the deliberative topics of honor, expediency, and their contraries for hortatory and dehortatory arguments.

They persuade to virtue (to put it simply) by extolling the celestial rewards of virtuous deeds; they incite their audience to seek true beatitude by describing the glories of heaven. Conversely, they attempt to dissuade their readers from pursuing worldly ends by exposing earthly felicity as false and transitory; they "dehort" from worldly affection by condemning its objects as ignoble and vain.

Finally, in several of these works, the flight sequence serves as a *consolatio*. In the writings of the Stoics, we have already encountered several of the motifs characteristic of these flight episodes: the felicity of virtuous souls after death, their delight in contemplating the heavens, and their scorn for the world and the bodies they have left behind. All these topics occur in Seneca's *To Polybius on Consolation*, where Seneca employs them primarily as arguments against grief. It is unreasonable (he concludes) to feel sorrow for a brother's death. If his soul has survived, he is blessed. If it has not survived, one is grieving for nothing: "Quid itaque eius desiderio maceror, qui aut beatus aut nullus est? Beatum inflere invidia est, nullum dementia."[31]

For both Stoics and Platonists, the soul's ascent to the heavens and its contempt for its narrow dwelling on earth served as arguments against passionate grief or fear. Since separation from the body is no evil, but an indispensable means of achieving felicity, the wise man ought neither to dread his own death nor to grieve for that of another. In the classical consolation, the flight motif accentuated the folly of those who mourn for the dead.

In three of these poems, the *Pharsalia*, the *Teseida*, and the *Troilus*, the flight episodes seem to retain this conventional association between the felicity of the dead and the folly of their mourners. Pompey finds occasion for mirth in the inadequate funeral rites performed by a grief-stricken follower. Troilus and Arcita ridicule the tears of their survivors. In all three instances the poet has employed commonplaces that had been frequently combined in the classical consolation. They will not (of course)

---

[31] Seneca, *Moral Essays*, II, 380. Pseudo-Aquinas alludes frequently to Seneca in his commentary on Boethius.

allay the sorrow of the fictional mourners within the poem (who are unaware of them); but they may nevertheless influence the writer's own audience, functioning as affective and logical proofs and mitigating the tragic effect of the hero's death.

In the *Commedia* and the *Somnium Scipionis* the connection with the *consolatio* is more tenuous, but it may not be altogether absent. Scipio simultaneously views the celestial reward that awaits him and learns that in the course of his short career on earth he must encounter envy, treachery, and an early death. In the *Paradiso* (in a passage strongly influenced by the *Somnium*), Dante is similarly warned by the glorified spirit of an ancestor that hostility and exile must be his lot. The misery he must expect on earth stands in forceful contrast to the felicity he now experiences in the skies and hopes to possess again as a *remuneratio aeterna*.

Thus far, I have attempted not only to reexamine Chaucer's flight passage in relation to the four analogues principally stressed by recent scholars, but to view it in its larger intellectual context, against the background of classical pneumatology and medieval commentary. Combining a variety of sciences and pseudosciences —cosmology and epistemology with astrology, ethics and metaphysics with eschatology—into a complex fusion of poetic convention and philosophical doctrine, this tradition displayed a comparable variety in mixing these diverse elements, oscillating between the extremes of imagination and reason, mythopoeic and logical thought. As the poetic apotheosis acquired Stoic and Platonic coloring, the ghost of the dead warrior assumed at times the features of the classical sage; and the journey of his spirit after death acquired a recognizable resemblance to the flight of the mind in contemplating the realm of ideas and the nature of things.

In the next chapters Troilus's ascent within the context of the poem itself will be considered, in examining its relationship to the Boethian insertions in the third and fourth books of Chaucer's romance and to Boethian or Christian commonplaces already explicit in the earlier version of the epilogue.

CHAPTER IV

BOETHIAN MONOLOGUE
AND PROPHETIC DREAM

In the Proem of the first book of the *Troilus*, while performing his divine (or profane) offices as Venus's clerk, the author bids the prayers of his audience on behalf of Love's servants. In the light of the poem as a whole, some of these prayers may seem prophetic:[1]

> And preieth for hem that ben in the cas
> Of Troilus, as ye may after here,
> That love hem brynge in hevene to solas; . . .
>
> Thus biddeth god, for his benignite,
> So graunte hem soone out of this world to pace,
> That ben despeired out of loves grace.

In the course of his double sorrow, Troilus himself frequently repeats the second of these behests, and his prayer is subsequently granted on the battlefield. The first prayer may be equivocal, and, if so, it is answered more than once: in his lady's arms and in his final ascent to the skies. If at first his "solas" is the conventional amorous pleasure of the lover, in the end it becomes remarkably similar to the consolation of philosophy.

We have already noted the transformation of the Elysium motif by Stoic and Neoplatonic philosophers and its influence on the flight sequences of the poets. Like the Boethian insertions in Books III and IV, Chaucer's flight stanzas represent a relatively late addition to his poem. Taken together, they heighten the dignity and the philosophical tenor of his romance, investing his chivalric stripling with an unexpected gravity more characteristic of Virgil's Orphic and Cicero's Neoplatonic protagonists or of Lucan's Stoic heroes. They bring into sharper focus the hero's

---

[1] Robert Kilburn Root, *The Book of Troilus and Criseyde* (Princeton, 1926), p. 4. Unless otherwise specified, all quotations from the *Troilus* are based on this edition.

intellectual development, the gradual evolution of his speculative powers toward the contemplative insight of the flight passage. They represent recognizable stages in Troilus's progress toward final illumination, and (though one cannot positively demonstrate that this was Chaucer's intent) there is a reasonable probability that he conceived them—like the stages of Boethius's own illumination in the *De Consolatione*—as phases in the progression from sensual ignorance to intellectual insight. Taken together, they broaden and deepen heroic decorum, complementing the love and valor of the chivalric hero with the promise (at least) of heroic wisdom. Without the two Boethian insertions,[2] the intellectual judgments that Troilus makes in the flight stanzas might seem inconsistent with his character as Chaucer had portrayed it earlier; by inserting these passages, the poet has laid the necessary foundations for the insights of the flight episode. The Boethian insertions function as preparation (*parasceve*) for the flight sequence, investing it with verisimilitude, consistency, and probability.

1

Of the principal characters in Chaucer's romance, Troilus alone discovers the nature of true felicity, and this he learns only with difficulty, through his personal experience of its contrary. The worldly Pandarus (who has hitherto failed as a lover) and the fearful Criseyde (who has already experienced adversity) are far more aware of the mutability of Fortune and the instability of her gifts—far more conscious of the brittleness of worldly delights —than is Troilus himself. Troilus is slow to recognize and reluctant to admit the inconstancy of Fortune, partly through youth and inexperience, but primarily perhaps because he himself is notably constant in his affection. The controlling irony of his

---

[2] On the Boethian monologues and Troilus's dream episode, see Walter Clyde Curry, *Chaucer and the Mediaeval Sciences*, rev. and enl. (New York, 1960), pp. 241-298, 343-348; Charles A. Owen, Jr., "The Significance of Chaucer's Revisions of *Troilus and Criseyde*," *MP*, LV (1957-1958), 105; Howard R. Patch, "Troilus on Determinism," *Speculum*, VI (1929), 225-243.

situation results from the fact that he—a constant lover himself —has not yet discovered a constant object for his love, an unchanging good wherein he may place his faith and fix his desire. This, by the very nature of things, does not and cannot exist on earth; he can find it only in the heavens. Paradoxically, in responding to a normal impulse of nature, he has not yet discovered either his own nature or the natural object of its desire. He is still (according to Boethian doctrine) a soul imprisoned in a body, a spark of celestial fire confined to the earth, and this can find its true and natural object only in the heavens whence it came. Troilus discovers his true nature and the true object of his desire only after separation from his body and its passions. Then, poised between the sublunary regions and the heavens, between the realm of generation and corruption and the realm immune to change, he can distinguish at last between mutable and immutable goods, between false and true felicity. Having remained constant in his devotion to an inconstant good through all vicissitudes of good and evil fortune, he achieves in the end a vision of absolute constancy.

Caught up in the wheel of change, the principal characters in this tragedy—and the doomed city of Troy itself—are not only ignorant of their true felicity but blind to the fact that the happiness they seek and the misery they strive to avoid are false. Along with the rest, Troilus hopes and fears, feels joy or sorrow for goods that are by nature mutable and transitory. These cloudy passions, traditionally condemned by the Stoics and equally distrusted by Boethius and the Platonists, obscure Troilus's reason no less than that of his companions and prevent him likewise from attaining true insight. Subtle though they are, his philosophical speculations fail to attain the mark; they fall significantly short of the conclusions at which Boethius himself was aiming. For all their Boethian echoes, neither of Troilus's philosophical monologues is a true consolation, and he does not experience the real "consolation of philosophy" or the real meaning of "stable faith" until he stands on the threshold of the heavens. Then, and only then, does he achieve a valid insight into the nature of true and false felicity.

The context of Troilus's hymn to Love in Book III is strikingly different from that of its source in the *Consolation* (Book II, meter 8). Troilus has just passed the night with Criseyde in the height of worldly bliss. He is at the apex of his prosperity. Boethius, however, languishes in prison, branded with infamy, accused of treason, and anticipating death. He has reached his lowest point on Fortune's wheel, and Philosophy is instructing him in the uses of adversity. It is the nature of Fortune to change (his tutor has just counseled him), and "contrarious Fortune profiteth more to men than Fortune debonayre."[3] Fortune varies her favors and disfavors, her alternations of prosperity and adversity, in accordance with universal law; "the world with stable feyth varieth accordable chaungynges."[4] Moreover, Philosophy's final verses in this song—"O weleful were mankynde, yif thilke love that governeth hevene governede yowr courages"—had been interpreted by at least one medieval writer (Pseudo-Aquinas) as an allusion to "divine love":[5]

O felix genus hominum supple. dico si amor scilicet divinus quo celum regitur regat animos vestros supple causando in eis amicitie concordiam.

In the end Troilus does apparently encounter *amor divinus*—but not yet, and not here—not in the house of a pander nor

---

[3] Boethius, Book II, prose 8. All quotations from Chaucer's translation of Boethius are derived from Robinson's edition.

[4] *Ibid.*, Book II, meter 8.

[5] Pseudo-Aquinas, Book II, meter 8, in *Boethius: Commentum duplex*: "In quo metro philosophia . . . primo commendat amorem divinum. Secundo ostendit quomodo humana natura amicitia conservatur." "primo di[cit] Amor sup. divinus regens terras ac pelagus et imperitans .i. frequenter imperans celo: ille amor ligat hanc seriem .i. concordiam rerum quod mundus stabili fide variat concordes vices .i. alternationes temporum anni noctis & diei." Cf. Trivet, fol. 137: "in hoc metro commendat amorem. et primo amorem divinum ostendens quomodo per ipsum conciliatur mundana concordia. secundo amorem hominum ostendens quomodo per ipsum conciliatur humana amicitia. . . ." "amor divinus quo producit & regit creaturas ligat hanc seriem .i. concordiam rerum qua mundus stabili fide i. iusto [*or* iuncto?] federe variat vices concordes .s. secundum e[adem?] tempora anni & alternacionem diei & noctis." "O felix genus hominum .s. dico esse. si amor quo celum regitur .i. amor divinus qui causat [*or* creat?] concordiam in celestibus regat animos vestros .s. causando in eis concordiam amicitie."

even in Criseyde's arms. He misses the logical force of Philosophy's verses: that the law of love governs the vicissitudes of Fortune, that the alternation of prosperity and adversity has been established by divine providence. He is blind to the relevance of this argument to his own situation; since he is now enjoying the height of earthly happiness, he should (according to the very passage Chaucer has adapted from the *De Consolatione*) anticipate a future change for the worse. He does not realize that the same "governaunce" of Love that has "joyned" him in "holsom alliaunce" with Criseyde will also disjoin them, that the stable law controlling the course of change will separate as well as combine, and that the same divine ordinance that has united the lovers will eventually divorce them. More significantly, he is unaware not only that the Love which now joins him to Criseyde will ultimately separate them but that it will, in the end, lead him back to his Creator. For (as Philosophy subsequently explains) the law of Love governs death as well as birth, corruption as well as generation, and will eventually restore all created beings to their first cause:[6]

And thus maketh Love entrechaungeable the perdurable courses; . . . This atempraunce norysscheth and bryngeth forth alle thinges that brethith lif in this world; and thilke same attempraunce, ravysschynge, hideth and bynymeth, and drencheth undir the last deth, alle things iborn. . . . This is the comune love to alle thingis, and alle thinges axen to ben holden by the fyn of good. For elles ne myghten they nat lasten yif thei ne comen nat eftsones ayein, by love retorned, to the cause that hath yeven hem beinge (*that is to seyn, to God*).

2

Chaucer's second Boethian insertion provides a forceful contrast to the first both in situation and in tone. Where the former monologue was lyrical, this is scholastic in style, heavily freighted with technical terms derived from Boethius's own philosophical vocabulary. Though this difference stems partly from Chaucer's

[6] Boethius, Book IV, meter 6.

source (in the first case a *metrum*, in the second a *prosa*), it is also psychologically and dramatically appropriate. Earlier, Troilus had given expression to his joy in a lyrical outburst; now, confronted by a sudden reversal in his fortunes and an alteration from the excess of bliss to utter despair, he is trying to reason his way out of his difficulty, to ascertain the cause of his tragedy. It is characteristic of him, perhaps, that he should focus his attention not so much on immediate causes as on loftier theological issues—problems of predestination and free will. On the former occasion Boethian *topoi* had adorned the raptures of his prosperity; now he turns to them for counsel in adversity.

Ironically, Troilus had already paraphrased the very lines with which Philosophy concludes her apology for Fortune, but without recognizing their true import. He had sung his hymn to Love in full confidence that his felicity would be permanent and his mistress constant in her affection. He had not realized that the love whereby "the world, with feith . . . that is stable, Diverseth so his stowndes concordynge"[7] is the divine law that governs the vicissitudes of Fortune and the temporal succession of all earthly things. He had not perceived that "al to litel . . . Lasteth swich joie" and that Fortune had beguiled him. When at last she does spin her wheel, he complains as bitterly as Boethius:

> . . . Fortune, allas the while! . . .
> Have I the nought honoured al my lyve,
> As thow wel woost, above the goddes alle?
> Whi wiltow me fro joie thus deprive? . . .
> O ye loveris, that heyghe upon the whiel
> Ben set of Fortune, in good aventure,
> God leve that ye fynde ay love of stiel,
> And longe mote youre lif in joie endure!

In his adversity, however, he realizes that there is a higher divinity than Fortune; and, after debating whether "forsight of divine purveyaunce Hath seyn alwey me to forgon Criseyde," he directs his prayer to the president of the immortals himself, to the supreme governor of the universe:

---

[7] *Troilus*, Book III, lines 1751-1752; cf. Boethius, Book II, meter 8.

> . . . almyghty Jove in trone
> That woost of al this thyng the sothfastnesse,
> Rewe on my sorwe, and do me deyen sone,
> Or bryng Criseyde and me fro this destresse.

In a sense both prayers are granted, His distressed lady will soon find solace in the arms of another lover. Troilus, in turn, destined (like Horatio) to absent himself from felicity a while, will "deyen sone" on the battlefield and learn to laugh at human sorrow.

In adversity and despair, both Troilus and Boethius complain against Fortune and turn to philosophy for an answer to their doubts. Both raise the question of divine providence and human freedom. Unlike the Roman senator, however, the Trojan warrior fails to achieve a satisfactory answer. After all, he has only Pandarus, not Dame Philosophy, to counsel him.

For Boethius, the answers to these questions constitute the final, and climactic, stage in his consolation. The "knowynge of thise thinges," his interlocutor informs him, "is a maner porcioun of the medycyne to the . . ."[8] Troilus never carries this argument through to its logical conclusion; his inner debate increases his doubt and exacerbates his grief instead of bringing consolation.

Having argued that the Unchangeable is the cause of all things that change—that the "engendrynge" and "progressiouns of muable nature" derive their causes, order, and forms, from "the stablenesse of the devyne thought," and that in different contexts men refer to the latter either as *purveaunce* or as *destyne*[9] —Philosophy resolves the conflict between free will and necessity, divine justice and divine foreknowledge, by stressing the difference between divine and human modes of knowledge: "alle thing that is iwist nis nat knowen by his nature propre, but by the nature of hem that comprehenden it. . . ."[10] In the final analysis, the result of this argument is to reaffirm the gulf between God and man, emphasizing the contrast between divine and human modes of knowledge and the antithesis between eternal and

[8] Boethius, Book IV, prose 6.
[9] *Ibid.*, Book IV, prose 6.
[10] *Ibid.*, Book V, prose 6.

temporal being. The development of Boethius's inquiry leads him beyond movement and change to a stable and unchanging Cause; beyond "temporel condicioun" to eternal insight; beyond the limitations of human nature and human reason to "the devyne nature and the devyne science." It leads him, in short, to God. Troilus's argument never reaches this end. He states the problem and develops it dialectically, advancing and refuting arguments pro and con, but fails to carry it through to its Boethian conclusion. He still remains ignorant of the quality of the divine nature and divine knowledge—of eternity as "parfit possessioun and altogidre of lif interminable"[11] —just as he is still unaware of his Highest Good, his final cause, and his "pleyn felicite."

Philosophy's reply to Boethius emphasizes the dignity as well as the limitations of human reason. In arguing that (contrary to common opinion) the objects of our knowledge are actually known and comprehended not through any power or force in themselves but "aftir the faculty (*that is to seyn, the power and the nature*) of hem that knowen,"[12] she correlates the various levels of human knowledge with particular faculties of the human mind, contrasting these not only with one another but with the divine intelligence. An object is comprehended differently by the sense ("wit"), the imagination, the reason, and the intelligence. Though the "resoun of mankynde" cannot approach the "simplicite of devyne prescience,"[13] it is a faculty that is unique to man and distinguishes him from the animals. Whereas the "wit of the body" and the imagination also belong to beasts, "resoun is al oonly to the lynage of mankynde, ryght as intelligence is oonly [to] the devyne nature."[14] Stressing the "upryght" stature that distinguishes man from beasts, Philosophy exhorts the "erthly man" who has waxed "yvel out of thi wit," to direct his thought to the heavens.[15]

---

[11] *Ibid*., Book V, prose 6.
[12] *Ibid*., Book V, prose 4.
[13] *Ibid*., Book V, prose 4.
[14] *Ibid*., Book V, prose 5.
[15] *Ibid*., Book V, meter 5.

As she has already explained,[16] free will is dependent on reason: "in alle thingis that resoun is, in hem also is liberte of willynge and of nillynge." This liberty is not, however "evenelyk in alle thinges," but varies in proportion to their freedom from the body and from bodily affections. In the "sovereynes devynes substaunces (*that is to seyn, in spiritz*) jugement is more cleer, and wil nat icorrumped, and myght redy to speden thinges that ben desired." The souls of men, in turn, are more free when they contemplate the mind of God, "whan thei loken hem in the speculacioun or lokynge of the devyne thought"; but they are "lasse fre whan thei slyden into the bodyes; and yit lasse fre whan thei ben gadrid togidre and comprehended in erthli membres. But the laste servage is whan that thei ben yeven to vices and han ifalle from the possessioun of hir propre resoun. For aftir that thei han cast awey hir eyghen fro the lyght of the sovereyn soth-fastnesse to lowe thingis and derke, anon thei derken by the cloude of ignoraunce and ben troubled by felonous talentz [appetites]; to the whiche talentz whan thei approchen and assenten, thei hepen and encrecen the servage which thei han joyned to hemself; and in this manere thei ben caytifs fro hir propre liberte."

This is the context of Boethius's questions concerning necessity and free will, and their significance depends partly on the discussion that precedes and follows them. When Chaucer transferred them from Boethius to Troilus, he inserted them into a very different context—a particular stage in the plot of a chivalric romance—and, though they did not entirely lose their former significance, they acquired further shades of meaning from this context. The lofty "questiouns of the symplicite of the purveaunce of God, and of the ordre of destyne, and of sodeyn hap, and of the knowynge and predestinacioun devyne, and of the liberte of fre wil"[17] must now appear relevant to the crisis of a despairing lover rather than to the intellectual and emotional dilemmas of a philosopher-statesman in disgrace with fortune and men's eyes.

[16] *Ibid.*, book V, prose 2.
[17] *Ibid.*, Book IV, prose 6.

They must now be interpreted in relation to the narrative plot of a medieval romance rather than to the logical and rhetorical structure of a Roman *consolatio*.

Troilus is no Boethius, of course. The chivalric hero and the classical moralist differ as profoundly as the works in which they appear. No less different are the occasions of their grief and the quality and objects of their passions. If Boethius's doctrine has successfully survived so violent a change in context, so radical a transplanting from one work to another, the reason lies partly in the fact that Chaucer's poem, like its source in Boccaccio, was already heavily saturated with Boethian doctrine. He could, accordingly, insert additional Boethian *topoi* without apparent violence to consistency and decorum. It was scarcely possible, however, to detach this argument entirely from its position in the logical development of Boethius's work, and the tension between its new and its original context created a potentially ironic situation that the poet might turn to his own advantage.

The recognition of what Boethius has said and Troilus leaves unsaid, the awareness of how the problem arose in the *De Consolatione* and how it was finally resolved, brings Troilus's own predicament into clearer focus. We are aware, as he is not, that to the lover's imagination and the "wit of the body" Criseyde's departure may present an appearance strikingly different from its aspect in the eye of human reason or in the comprehensive and simultaneous vision of the divine intelligence. We are aware, as Troilus is not, that he has been guided by imagination and sense—by the wit of the body—rather than by rational judgment. We are aware, as he is not, that his reason has been partially obscured and his will partly enslaved by the passions of the body. Finally, we are conscious, as he is not, of the greater clarity of judgment and greater freedom of will that the soul may achieve after its separation from "erthli membres" and its return to the "lyght of the sovereyn sothfastnesse." Chaucer has prepared us for his hero's final apotheosis; when at length Troilus returns to the heavens, his vision of "pleyn felicite" may arouse surprise, but should seem neither inconsistent nor improbable.

The second Boethian insertion stands midway between Troilus's hymn to Love and his apotheosis. Taken together, these three passages reveal his gradual progess toward "heroic knowledge." Like the first insertion, this second Boethian monologue is incomplete. In the first instance Troilus's misinterpretation of Boethian doctrine and, in the second, his failure to pursue the argument to its conclusion underscore his mortal ignorance; they emphasize his limited knowledge rather than his philosophical insight. In the first case, however, he remains unaware of his error; in the second, he at least knows that he does not know.

3

Though Troilus asks the right questions, he does not find the right answers, and the total result of his questioning is to enhance the irony of his predicament: that ignorance of self and situation that, for Chaucer and Boethius alike, constitutes the fundamental irony of the *condition humaine*. In the *Troilus* this is exemplified not only in the fate of the protagonists themselves but in the tragic destiny that overhangs their city. But for the imminent doom of Troy, there would presumably have been no love affair between Troilus and Criseyde and no separation. Both events are made possible by Calkas's foreknowledge of his city's destruction and his desertion to the Greeks. Criseyde herself unwittingly functions as an instrument of destiny in accomplishing Troy's doom. The exchange of prisoners that restores her to her father simultaneously restores Antenor to Troy; the city is now vulnerable to his future treachery. Moreover, if Chaucer (like Boccaccio) regarded Criseyde as primarily responsible for Troilus's death, she had (it would seem) further hastened her city's doom by depriving it of its chief bulwark; as a warrior Troilus is second only to Hector. Her very fear and her desire for a protector help to precipitate the catastrophe.

Troilus is correct, apparently, in attributing Criseyde's departure to Fortune and to the providence of Jove, but he does not and cannot perceive the divine purpose underlying the exchange of prisoners. As Chaucer informs us in the context of Hector's death and Troilus's end:

> Fortune, which that permutacioun
> Of thynges hath, as it is hire committed
> By purveyaunce and disposicioun
> Of heigh Jove, as regnes shal be flitted
> Fro folk to folk, or whan they shal ben smytted,
> Gan pulle awey the fetheres brighte of Troie
> Fro day to day, til they ben bare of joie.

This is sound Boethian doctrine, and its application to the destiny of Troy is as valid as for Boethius's own predicament. If there is tragic irony in Troilus's own speculations on providence, it springs from his inability to perceive the divine intent that underlies his mistress's departure and its significance for his city's fate. Like Hector's death, Criseyde's return to her father is inextricably linked with Troy's destruction. It not only speeds Antenor back to Ilium, but fills her royal lover with the desire for death. The very despair that prompts Troilus's soliloquy, his will to die, the death that overtakes him so soon after Hector's fate in (traditionally) so similar a manner—these too must be seen as part of the divine strategy for the overthrow of Troy.

4

Though the *Filostrato* does not describe Hector's death, Chaucer introduces this episode into the closely linked chain of events that, beginning with Troilus's dream, culminates in his recognition of Criseyde's infidelity—a recognition that, like many other tragic discoveries, will have fatal consequences. Troilus has already repeatedly expressed the wish to die, and upon learning the truth he becomes (unlike Claudio) absolute for death:

> Myn owen deth in armes wol I seche;
> I recche nat how soone be the day.

In Troilus's recognition of the brooch, as in the dream itself, the reader may detect the directing hand of Providence. In both of these incidents, as in the exchange of prisoners and the death of Hector, the gods themselves have intervened to destroy Troilus's happiness and thereby remove the chief remaining pillar of the Trojan state. As Troilus has correctly surmised, his dream had been divinely sent:

> My lady bright, Criseyde, hath me bytrayed,
> In whom I trusted most of any wight;
> The blisful goddes, thorugh hire grete myght,
> Han in my drem yshewed it ful right.

> He thoughte ay wel he hadde his lady lorn,
> And that Joves, of his purveyaunce,
> Hym shewed hadde in slep the signifiaunce
> Of hire untrouthe and his disaventure. . . .

Though Troilus's identification of the brooch is described as "a cas" and a "newe chaunce," the poet's Boethian frame of reference leaves no room for chance; fortune and fate alike are firmly under the control of providence. In this context, the allusions to Hector's fate and Troy's destruction obliquely emphasize the "first cause" of the discovery sequence. They give additional clarity to the providential role of the gods in exposing Criseyde's guilt and precipitating her lover's death. Less than three hundred lines separate Chaucer's reference to the "fyn of the parodie" of Hector from the poet's reflections on Troilus's unhappy "fyn". The lines describing Hector's encounter with nemesis may apply with equal validity to the discovery sequence:

> The fate wolde his soule sholde unbodye,
> And shapen hadde a mene it out to dryve;
> Ayeyns which fate hym helpeth nat to stryve; . . .

The dream and the brooch alike are instruments of providence: "menes" divinely contrived to "unbodye" Troilus's soul and hasten Troy's destruction.

The discovery sequence antedates Chaucer's major insertions in the three final books. Most of its principal episodes had been derived, in part at least, from the *Filostrato*, and in the unrevised *Troilus* some of them already possessed substantial links with several of the principal motifs of the original epilogue—the infidelity of earthly lovers, the transiency of worldly joys, the faithfulness of divine love. On the whole, however, Chaucer's insertions significantly altered the original context of the discovery sequence. Occupying an intermediate position between Troilus's soliloquy on divine foreknowledge and his ascent to the heavens, it not only develops themes that had already been elaborated in Troilus's meditation, but also points forward to insights he would later achieve in Elysium. In this altered context, the discovery sequence complements Troilus's speculations on providence by positively demonstrating the divine origin of his dream, the validity of Cassandra's interpretation, and the infallibility of divine testimony. Similarly, by finally opening his eyes to the fact of Criseyde's inconstancy, it prepares him (as well as the reader) for his vision of stable and permanent bliss. Even in the unrevised *Troilus* his discovery of his lady's faithlessness would have been thematically linked with the epilogue; by inserting the flight stanzas, Chaucer reinforced these ties. In the revised *Troilus,* the epilogue, like the discovery scene itself, centers on the hero's own act of recognition. On the former occasion he achieved an insight into infidelity: knowledge of an unstable and inconstant Good; on the latter occasion, insight into transcendent faithfulness: knowledge of a constant and steadfast Good. Both are valid insights, and in a sense they are complementary. For Chaucer, as for Boethius, knowledge of falsehood was preliminary to knowledge of truth; recognition of false felicity, a precondition for realization of true beatitude.

The revised *Troilus* ends, then, with two complementary recognition scenes. In the first, after doubts and misgivings, the protagonist finally realizes his mistress's unfaithfulness. In the second, he recognizes the distinction between temporal and eternal, earthly and celestial goods. He perceives the vanity of the whole world in comparison with the full felicity of heaven.

Like the Boethian soliloquy in Book IV, Chaucer's dream episode heightens the contrast between human ignorance and divine knowledge. As on the former occasion, he develops the potentialities for irony inherent in Troilus's own situation—and in the human condition itself—through raising the issue of divine providence and (more specifically) through centering this episode on the problem of knowledge. What does the dream signify? Was it really sent by the gods? Is Criseyde indeed untrue? Like the gods, the reader knows the answers to these questions, but Troilus does not; the irony and pathos of his situation are heightened by our awareness that he has already received the true answers but has ignorantly cast them aside. The process of retrieving them, of regaining the insights he had already possessed, is painful, but it is a return to reason. As the narcotic effects of Pandarus's consolations and Criseyde's flattering lies begin to wear off, as suspicion and despair revive, he awakens at length (like a patient after a serious operation) to the full realization of his "wo." Though he wakes only to the consciousness of his lady's falsehood and his own despair, this too is valid knowledge.

As the reader is well aware, the dream was a direct warning from the gods; in doubting it Troilus has in effect shifted his trust from the testimony of the gods to that of his faithless mistress, from the admonition of divine providence to the worldly prudence of his friend, that *homme moyen sensuel*. After first believing this divine revelation, Troilus suppresses his own misgivings, places his faith in the protestations of Pandarus and Criseyde, and indignantly rejects a second divine warning—the testimony of the inspired "Sibille his suster." After Hector's death, Troilus begins all over again to suspect the truth, "And dradde ay that his lady was untrewe." Nevertheless, he is still a model lover, and, "as thise loveres don," he continues to excuse her. Even though her final letter impresses him as "a kalendes of chaunge," he still hopes that she will keep her word:

> For with ful yvel wil list hym to leve
> That loveth wel, in swich cas, though hym greve.

Only his recognition of the brooch opens his eyes to "the sothe."

Troilus recognizes only "at the laste" what the reader and the gods have known all along: that Criseyde has played him false. Heaven has spoken truth, and the men who doubted its message have been proven demonstrably wrong. As Troilus learns to his own despair, Criseyde has lied and Pandarus has erred. Virtually the entire discovery sequence centers on an epistemological issue—the conflict between divine and human testimony—and the focal point of this conflict is the significance of the hero's dream. The contradictory opinions expressed by Pandarus and Cassandra as to its validity accentuate the antithesis between human fallibility and divine truth. Indeed, the fact that Cassandra has been destined to speak truly yet be disbelieved gives additional force to this contrast. (Chaucer had, in fact, altered Boccaccio's account in order to assign to Cassandra, rather than to Troilus, the explanation of his dream.) Troilus himself has held discordant opinions; his vacillations between belief and disbelief in the dream, between doubt and faith in Criseyde's word, reflect the conventional *ethos* and *pathos* of the lover, but they also reveal his capacity for self-deception.

In contrast to Criseyde's infidelity and Pandarus's misguidance, the faithfulness of the gods has been clearly demonstrated. The dream episode and the recognition scene indirectly prepare the reader for Troilus's final insight into the stable faith that governs the heavens (a Boethian doctrine that he had "fumbled" in his hymn in Book III): his insight into the distinction between earthly and celestial values, temporal and eternal goods, constant and inconstant felicity.

Thus far, we have considered the flight passage in relation to the Boethian insertions in Books III and IV and to the discovery sequence in the latter part of Book V. In this section, completed before all three of these insertions, Chaucer had developed with fine irony the predominant role of providence in bringing about the catastrophe of the poem. He had explicitly linked Hector's nemesis with that of Troy, attributing both disasters to fate or providence. Hector and Troilus are parallel figures, not only brothers but the best warriors in Troy; both have been defenders of Criseyde; both perish at the hands of Achilles. From the role of providence in Troilus's bitter discovery and Hector's death, the reader could scarcely avoid inferring that Troilus's death also has been divinely contrived.

As the poem originally stood, the meditation on Troilus's end followed immediately after the account of his "pitous" death. There was no compensatory flight to the skies, no vision of full felicity, no laughter at the grief of mourners, no contempt of the world or condemnation of transitory pleasures from the viewpoint of the heavens. Troilus had died the violent death he had prayed for, and that was all.

For a reader who recalled the circumstances of Hector's "fyn" some three hundred lines earlier, and the role of fate in "shaping" it, the poet's reflections on Troilus's "fyn" must leave a bitter taste. They could scarcely fail to place fate, and the divine providence that had determined it, in a harsh and cruel light. Troilus, Hector, and Criseyde herself had all (it would seem) been dispensable pawns in a cosmic chess game, calculated losses in Jove's scheme for Troy's destruction. The original epilogue did little to counter this harsh impression; perhaps this was one of the considerations that induced Chaucer to insert the flight stanzas and to raise the issue of providence in the Boethian monologue of Book IV. Both, in fact, serve to correct and mitigate the one-sided picture of providence which emerges from the unrevised *Troilus*. The Boethian passage from which Chaucer derived Troilus's soliloquy attempts to reconcile free will with predestination in order to establish man's moral responsibility for his own actions and to vindicate divine justice in apportioning rewards and penalties. The flight episode in turn brings Troilus to "pleyn felicite," thus giving an additional significance to his "fyn," and the circumstances that led to his death now appear in a double light. If on the one hand providence has contrived his death in order to destroy Troy (the pun is Chaucer's own), on the other hand it has ruined his earthly happiness to bring him to true beatitude. Chaucer has thus complemented and extended his original image of providence, shifting his emphasis from its destructive aspect to its role in salvation.

Similarly exploiting the ironies inherent in popular and learned conceptions of mortality, he has placed death itself in a more favorable light. For Stoics, Platonists, and Christian theologians alike, death was a good, not an evil; separation from the body was a prerequisite for the full felicity of the soul. Chaucer had already described Hector's death as the separation of body and soul ("The fate wolde his soule sholde unbodye . . ."), recounting Troilus's "sorwe" and "wo" on that occasion. He had not, however, specified the destination of Hector's spirit or cast doubts on the reasonableness of Troilus's grief. Nor had he raised the issue of whether Hector's fate should be regarded as good or evil.

In the flight sequence, however, he returns to these topics. What the separation of body and soul really means—for the classical philosopher, as for the Christian theologian—becomes evident in Troilus's "blissful" contemplation of the heavens and his laughter at the mourners about his body. Neither philosophers nor theologians, these grieving Trojans (fated to die themselves in so short a time) naïvely regard death as an evil. Troilus had earlier felt similar grief for Hector and (albeit for different reasons) intenser sorrow for Criseyde. The ridicule he directs toward the laments of his friends emphasizes the insignificance of his own past sufferings. The single outburst of ghostly laughter reduces the entire tale of his double sorrows to its true proportions: a point of time on a "litel spot of erthe." From the threshold of the heavens, his own lament for Hector and his multiple sorrows for Criseyde would seem as ridiculous as the tears of his survivors. Troilus's laughter at death and human grief alike has reduced to insignificance the last grounds for complaint against the providence and just dispensation of the gods.

CHAPTER V

FELICITY AND MUTABILITY: BOETHIAN FRAMEWORK OF THE *TROILUS*

For Dante, Boethius was "the sainted soul, which unmasketh the deceitful world." A luminary of the Christian church, he had died a martyr's death, and leaving his body to be buried in Pavia, had been glorified in the sun. In the company of Saint Thomas Aquinas and other theologians, he now enjoyed the vision of "every good":[1]

> Per vedere ogni ben, dentro vi gode
> L'anima santa che 'l mondo fallace
> Fa manifesto a chi di lei ben ode.

> Lo corpo ond' ella fu cacciata giace
> Giuso in Cieldauro, ed essa da martiro
> E da essilio venne a questa pace.

Dante's admiration for the *De Consolatione* is reflected in echoes of this work throughout the *Commedia*, but its influence is particularly striking in his relations with Beatrice. His continuous dialogue with the personification of sacred theology—the *divina scientia* which teaches the true blessedness of man and the way to achieve it—is analogous to Boethius's discourse with Dame Philosophy. Many of the same *topoi* would recur in the *Troilus*: the contrast between the fate of the body and that of the soul (extending even to the violent death that "drives" or "chases" the immortal spirit from its mortal vehicle), the contrast between the "false world" and the vision of "every good," and the antithesis between earthly and celestial felicity. Appropriately Dante begins his next canto with a Boethian *topos* ("O insensata cura de' mortali"). Echoing Philosophy's condemnation of humanity's pre-occupation with temporal things, he contrasts the joys of heaven with worldly cares—legal studies, pursuit of wealth and power,

---

[1] Grandgent, pp. 748-749; Carlyle-Wicksteed, p. 465.

delights of the flesh. It is within the same Boethian frame of reference and in much the same spirit that Chaucer contrasts the full felicity of heaven with the vanity of the wretched world and its transitory lust. Like Dante's worldlings, Chaucer's hero is "nel diletto de la carne involto."[2]

Since Chaucer's debt to Boethius has already received intensive analysis from others, we shall reconsider this problem only insofar as it has relevance for the flight stanzas. Curry's charge that the epilogue is inconsistent with the rest of the *Troilus* scarcely does justice either to Chaucer's artistry or to the evidence of the text. If one condemns the epilogue as inconsistent with the romantic values of the plot, one can hardly avoid finding similar inconsistencies in the moral reflections that recur throughout the poem either in the poet's own person or through his *dramatis personae*. In the last analysis, Criseyde's reflections on the instability of worldly joy, Pandarus's observations on Fortune's changes, and Chaucer's repeated allusions to fortune and chance or fate and providence represent partial and incomplete statements of doctrines that will receive clearer and fuller expression in the epilogue. Like the epilogue, they are an integral part of the Boethian context of Chaucer's romance.

The alleged inconsistency of the epilogue (it would seem) actually springs from Chaucer's conscious juxtaposition of two different but complementary points of view: the naive and worldly attitude toward earthly prosperity and adversity, and the heavenly teachings of philosophy. The former belongs to opinion, the latter to knowledge. In Boethius's dialogue these contrasting attitudes are initially represented by the narrator and Dame Philosophy. Conventional in classical and medieval thought, this antithesis underlies the epistemological structure of the *Troilus* and much of the poet's finest irony.

The flight stanzas themselves represent a fusion of Boethian *topoi* with the apotheosis motif of the poets and the pneumato-

---

[2] Grandgent, pp. 752-753; Carlyle-Wicksteed, p. 469.

logy of Stoic and Neoplatonic philosophers.[3] Though Troilus's condemnation of the world's transitory "lust" and his vision of the "pleyn felicite" of heaven are essentially Boethian, other motifs—the contemplation of heaven and earth, the comparison of the magnitude of the one with the insignificance of the other, the derision of earthly affections, and indeed the ascent motif itself—are common to all three of these traditions. Moreover, besides the commonplaces shared by the works themselves, medieval exegesis had forged additional links. Commentators had interpreted Boethius in the light of the same philosophical doctrines they had brought to the explication of Lucan and Cicero and Dante. In introducing his flight sequence into a poem already heavily permeated with Boethian thought, Chaucer was not patching an old garment with new or different material; he was adding like to like.

In one respect there is a significant difference between Boethius's flight metaphors and Troilus's ascent. The former refer essentially to the ascent of the mind in contemplation; the latter represents the journey of the soul after death. Different as they

---

[3] On the problem of the sources of Boethius's doctrines—Stoic, Platonic, Aristotelian, or Christian—see Fritz Klingner, "De Boethii *Consolatione Philosophiae*," *Philologische Untersuchungen*, vol XXVII (Berlin, 1921); E. K. Rand, "On the Composition of Boethius' *Consolatio Philosophiae*," *Harvard Studies in Classical Philology*, XV (1904), 1-28; G. A. Mueller, "Die Trostschrift des Boetius, Beitrag zu einer literarhistorischen Quellenuntersuchung" (Ph. D. diss., Berlin, 1912); Jan Sulowski, "Les sources du *De consolatione Philosophiae* de Boèce," *Sophia*, XXV (1957), 76-85; Sulowski, "The Sources of Boethius' *De consolatione Philosophiae*," *Sophia*, XXIX (1961), 67-94; E. T. Silk, "Boethius's *Consolatio Philosophiae* as a Sequel to Augustine's Dialogues and Soliloquia," *Harvard Theological Review*, XXXIII (1939), 19-39; Howard R. Patch, "Fate in Boethius and the Neoplatonists," *Speculum*, IV (1929), 62-72; Patch, "Necessity in Boethius and the Neoplatonists," *Speculum*, X (1935), 393-404; Volker Schmidt-Kohl, *Die neuplatonische Seelenlehre in der "Consolatio Philosophiae" des Boethius*, *Beiträge zur Klassischen Philologie*, Heft 16 (Meisenheim am Glan, 1965); Pierre Courcelle, *La Consolation de Philosophie dans la Tradition Littéraire, Antécédents et Postérité de Boèce* (Paris, 1967). See also Willy Theiler, "Antike und christliche Rückkehr zu Gott," in *Mullus, Festschrift Theodor Klausner* (Münster, 1964), pp. 352-361.

are, however, the two genres are interrelated. Like the felicity of philosophers in this life, the beatitude of separated souls after death consists primarily in contemplation. For the later Stoics, with their bent for natural philosophy, this was contemplation of the heavens. For the Neoplatonists, it was contemplation of the realm of Ideas and the vision of divine beauty or the Supreme Good. For Christian theologians, it was the beatific vision, the *visio Dei*. The fact that the two genres shared the same imagery and frequently the same doctrines made it easier to combine them in a single work. Thus the analogies between Troilus's flight and the speculative ascent enabled Chaucer to draw not only on the posthumous flight of Pompey's soul and the visionary ascents of Dante and Scipio but also on the speculative flight imagery of Boethius.

In recent years the Boethian content of the *Troilus*[4] and its broader intellectual background have been subjected to detailed analysis. In Professor Robinson's opinion, Chaucer's translation of the *Consolation* "unquestionably" reveals the influence not only of the Latin original but of "the Latin commentary of Nicholas Trivet and a French prose version ascribed to Jean de Meun." Whether Chaucer also knew the commentary by Pseudo-Aquinas is uncertain. Parallels formerly cited as evidence for such indebtedness seem to point instead to the influence of Trivet's commentary; moreover, in Robinson's view, this was "probably" a source of Pseudo-Aquinas's commentary.[5]

[4] See chap. iii, n. 3, on Chaucer's indebtedness to Boethius.

[5] F. N. Robinson, *The Works of Geoffrey Chaucer*, 2d ed. (Boston, 1957), p. 797. The commentaries by Guillaume de Conches and Nicholas Trivet are available in the MLA Collection of Photographic Facsimiles, nos. 99 and 100. Relevant portions of Trivet's commentary have been summarized or quoted by D. W. Robertson in *A Preface to Chaucer: Studies in Medieval Perspectives* (Princeton, 1963), pp. 24-27, 358-360, and *passim*. For the uncertainty attending the date of Pseudo-Aquinas's commentary, cf. Kate O. Petersen, "Chaucer and Trivet," *PMLA*, XVIII (1903), 174; examining over 370 parallels, Petersen (pp. 175-176) finds about 70 cases in which Pseudo-Aquinas fails to "give as close a correspondence with Chaucer's text as Trivet's comedy does." For discussion of the commentaries on the *Consolatio* from the ninth

In considering the Boethian element in Chaucer's romance, I shall not attempt a detailed analysis of sources and analogues. Instead I shall limit this study to general observations on the Boethian tradition, noting its relevance for the genre of Chaucer's poem, for his treatment of character and passion, and for the tragic end of his hero, followed by the final glimpse of true felicity. Pseudo-Aquinas's commentary will be treated less as a potential source than as a significant statement of the medieval Boethian tradition. Representing a stage of development apparently later than Trivet's work, it brings us closer to the *De Consolatione* of Chaucer's contemporaries. Finally, I shall examine some of the principal Boethian *topoi* of the flight episode, noting similarities and dissimilarities between the Boethian and Lucanic traditions.

1

In the Monk's definition of tragedy, recent scholarship has not only detected the influence of medieval glosses on Boethius's reference to tragedy but has rightly stressed the significance of this influence for the *Troilus*.[6] In accordance with contemporary ideas of tragedy, Chaucer recounts his medieval tale as though it were a true history rather than a fictitious argument, appealing to the testimony of his nonexistent author Lollius. The tragedy of Troilus is, he pretends, a "storie" recorded in "olde bookes," not simply a fiction invented by a twelfth-century poet and elaborated by thirteenth- and fourteenth-century authors. Like other tragic

---

century through the fifteenth, see Courcelle, *La Consolation de Philosophie.* The authorship of Pseudo-Aquinas's commentary has been variously ascribed to William Whetley, Thomas Waleis, and "un certain Marquand" (possibly Marquand the Scot, who was rector of the University of Paris around the middle of the fourteenth century); Courcelle, pp. 322-323.

[6] See Robertson, *A Preface to Chaucer*, pp. 346, 472-474, 495, 500; Robertson, "Chaucerian Tragedy," *ELH*, XIX (1952), 1-37; Walter Clyde Curry, *Chaucer and the Mediaeval Sciences* (New York, 1960), pp. 241, 281-294; Willard Farnham, *The Medieval Heritage of Elizabethan Tragedy* (New York, 1956), pp. 129-172; Patch, "Troilus on Determinism," *Speculum*, VI, (1929), 225-243.

protagonists, the hero stands "in greet prosperitee," falls "Into myserie, and endeth wrecchedly," a reversal underlined by the poet's frequent references to Fortune's changes and the hero's sorrows and by final reflections on Troilus's unhappy end. Moreover, like two of the Monk's "illustrious men"—Samson and Hercules—Troilus meets his death through his "lemman," an end that is all the more tragic inasmuch as the hero, like the conventional suicide, seeks his own death through despair.

There is, nevertheless, one significant difference: Troilus is not "yfallen out of heigh degree." He enjoys the renown of a warrior and the wealth and dignities of a royal prince until the end; then he perishes not ingloriously on the battlefield, the very kind of death that other poets had celebrated in heroic verse. The prosperity and misery he encounters, the changes of Fortune he experiences—these are the conventional vicissitudes of a lover rather than of a tragic hero; other poets had treated such materials comically or elegiacally and on occasion Chaucer does so himself. Chaucer has taken the transiency of worldly love rather than the loss of worldly dignities and high estate as his subject matter, but he has invested this erotic content with the shape and structure of tragedy. Though the Trojan war provides a tragic context for the history of the lovers, though their end is tragic and they themselves belong to the rank appropriate for tragedy, much of Chaucer's material, as he must have realized, was the conventional matter of comedy; in particular, the triadic relation of lover, bawd, and mistress had been traditionally associated with the comic genre.[7] In placing the joys and suf-

---

[7] For medieval theories of comedy and tragedy, see Marvin T. Herrick, *Comic Theory in the Sixteenth Century* (Urbana, 1964), pp. 57-70; Madeleine Doran, *Endeavors of Art: A Study of Form in Elizabethan Drama* (Madison, 1964), pp. 105-109; J. E. Spingarn, *A History of Literary Criticism in the Renaissance* (New York, 1925), pp. 65-67; Willi Erzgräber, "Tragik und Komik in Chaucer's *Troilus and Criseyde*," *Festschrift für Walter Hübner*, ed. Dieter Riesner and Helmut Gneuss (Berlin, 1964), pp. 139-163. On the mixture of comic and serious elements in medieval epic and the "principle *ludicra seriis miscere*," see Ernst Robert Curtius, *European Literature and the Latin Middle*

ferings of the lovers against the background of the imminent doom of Troy,[8] Chaucer juxtaposed a historical theme universally recognized as tragic in the highest degree and an erotic subject that might embrace not only the heroic values of chivalric romance but also the humbler values of comedy and the sentimental values of elegy.

The problem of the genres appropriate to secular erotic themes demands fuller discussion than one can accord it here. In classical or medieval literature, the subject of *amor* might occur in such diverse art forms as epic or pastoral, comedy or tragedy, elegy or satire, encomium or didactic verse treatise. The treatment of this theme varied, moreover, with genre. In tragedy it might be presented pejoratively, as a passion leading to madness or death. In epic it might serve either as a spur or as a check to heroic actions—an incentive to the pursuit of glory or a temptation to ignoble ease.

Though medieval poetic theory usually assigned warfare to tragedy (and/or epic), and love and marriage to comedy, this

---

Ages, trans. Willard R. Trask (New York and Evanston, 1963), pp. 428-431. As Curtius points out (p.429), Servius found elements of the comic style in book IV of the *Aeneid*: "Est autem paene totus in affectione, licet in fine pathos habeat, ubi abscessus Aeneae gignit dolorem. Sane totus in consiliis et subtilitatibus est: nam paene comicus stilus est: nec mirum ubi de amore tractatur." For a medieval reader, the mixture of comic and tragic elements in Chaucer's poem might seem consistent with Vergil's practice in the *Aeneid*. Common to both tragedies would be the Trojan nationality of the hero and the theme of Troy's destruction, the contrast between faithful and unfaithful lover (an antithesis developed in Chaucer's account of Dido and Aeneas in the *House of Fame* and the *Legend of Good Women*), the seriocomic treatment of a love affair, and the tragic death of the faithful partner. Just as Dido's *dolor* springs from *abscessus Aeneae*, Troilus's grief is renewed by the departure of Criseyde.

[8] On the Trojan background of the *Troilus*, see Charles A. Owen, "The Significance of Chaucer's Revisions of *Troilus and Criseyde*," *MP*, LV (1957-1958), 1-5; Bloomfield, "Distance and Predestination," pp. 14-26; Theodore A. Stroud, "Boethius' Influence on Chaucer's *Troilus*," *MP*, XLIX (1951-1952), 1-9; John P. McCall, "The Trojan Scene in Chaucer's *Troilus*," *ELH*, XXIX (1962), 263-275; Robert D. Mayo, "The Trojan Background of the *Troilus*," *ELH*, IX (1942), 245-256.

distinction was based essentially on the correlation between literary genre and social level. While the deeds of noble or "courtly" persons demanded the epic or tragic genre and the resources of the high style, the actions of the middle or lower classes were more appropriate for comedy and for the middle or low styles. Although Dante associates the theme of love (*Venus*) with *salus* and *virtus* as subjects meriting an "illustrious" and "courtly" tongue, the majority of medieval literary theorists, heavily dependent on late classical rhetoric and poetic, failed to give adequate consideration to the medieval vogue of courtly lyric and romance. Medieval poetics already possessed a theory concerning the genre and style appropriate for depicting the military exploits of a man in high estate and for portraying the sudden alterations of fortune that could change his prosperity into disaster. It had not, however, managed to evolve a systematic and coherent theory concerning the genre and style best suited for a description of his love affairs or for an expression of his passion. Though rhetorical treatises and *artes poeticae* might regard love (among other emotions) as an *affectus* especially appropriate to youth, they rarely developed this point; they considered it primarily in relation to personal attributes (*attributa personarum*) and to the requirements of decorum in character. They failed, on the whole, to come to grips with the problem of how to portray a lover of noble rank and how to differentiate his emotions and his behavior under the influence of *eros* from those of a man of meaner station. It was left to the poets, in large part, to raise and resolve such questions for themselves.

In contrast with the large body of chivalric romances and courtly lyrics devoted to the amours of the nobility, literary theorists tended to neglect this theme. Though their omission may prove a source of embarrassment to the modern scholar, it nevertheless left considerable latitude to the medieval poet. Since the essential factor determining the choice of the comic or tragic genre was the social level of the characters portrayed, the writer of courtly romance might combine the motifs of love and valor, incorporating elegaic or even comic elements into his account of the lover's fortunes without altering its genre. Whether it portrayed arms or amours, his *roman* retained its affinities with epic (or narrative "tragedy"), inasmuch as its protagonists were ladies and cavaliers of "gentle" birth and rank. In the same way, Chaucer's romance of Troilus's ill-starred passion remains an epic "tragedy," even though it contains elements of comedy, elegy, and encomium. As in Virgil's *alta tragedia* and as in the medieval romances of Tristan and Lancelot, the themes of love and valor and ruin are interwoven. Troilus's passion, like that of Dido and Achilles and Paris and so many other classical and medieval heroes or heroines, terminates in death.

In this context we may also recall the conventional distinction between elegy and tragedy in subject matter and style. According to one early Renaissance commentator, tragic and heroic poetry concern grave personages and arduous actions and require the high style. It is "inept" to employ the high and heroic style for miserable things or to treat great or magnificent things in the elegiac mode. The amours of hopeless or perishing lovers are appropriate for elegy, but magnificent things belong to heroic poetry:[9]

Est autem tam in metro quam in prosa triplex dicendi qualitas seu stilus seu genus. Aliud enim genus dicitur altiloquum seu sublime: & competit personis dignis & rebus arduis. Qualia sunt heroica & tragica carmina: & omnes de republica: . . . Oportet preterea ut sit uniforme generi poematis. Qui enim de rebus miseris loquens heroico stilo & altiloquo genere utatur: aut de rebus magnificis elegiaco multum ineptiret. Res enim misere ut amores misere depereuntium: epitaphia & eiusmodi elegis scribi volunt: res magnifice heroicis carminibus.

Such considerations as these did not, of course, alter the genre of the *Troilus*, but they did at times bring Chaucer's tragedy close to the frontiers of comedy and elegy without actually violating them. They made it possible for him to include some of his finer comic scenes within the context of a tragic fable, to give lyric expression to the joys and sorrows of the lovers, and, finally, to introduce a tragicomic element into the account of his hero's death.

The flight episode itself brings into sharper focus the under-

---

[9] Ascensius, "Proemium," in *Boethius: Commentum duplex.*

lying ambiguities in Chaucer's ironic "tragedye." Pompey's death had been genuinely tragic, Arcita's slightly less so. By inserting the flight stanzas after the account of Troilus's death, Chaucer strengthened the link between his own "tragedye" and those of Lucan and Boccaccio. At the same time, however, he gave clearer definition to the comic values already inherent in his poem. In Chaucer's romance, with its rich comic overtones, the hero's laughter acquires a force and a relevance that it could not have achieved in the *Pharsalia* (which exhibits a fine sense of irony but little sense of comedy) or even in the *Teseida*.

Already established in the poetry of Lucan and Boccaccio, the motif of the hero's posthumous laughter reinforces Chaucer's tragic (or epic) decorum, yet it also accentuates the comic element already strongly enunciated in his work. The basis for this paradoxical relationship to two contrasting genres and literary modes is to be found in the doctrinal systems—Stoic and Platonic, Boethian and Christian—underlying all three of these flight episodes. That a tension between tragic and comic values underlies Chaucer's entire poem; that, though the tragic sense predominates in the plot, it is the comic vision that overcomes in the end; that, in the light of Troilus's final insight, secular tragedy itself vanishes into insignificance, and worldly prosperity and adversity seem equally negligible—this is a poetic heresy perhaps, but from the vantage point of Philosophy, it may be a divine orthodoxy.

2

It was difficult for a poet to take Boethius piecemeal. Though the *Consolation* would hardly meet Husserl's conditions for philosophy as *strenge Wissenschaft*, it is nevertheless a closely reasoned, tightly structured work centering upon the vision of an eternal good as true felicity and culminating in the idea of divine providence as an eternal present. To detach a single concept, such as Boethius's Fortune, from the whole and develop it in isolation from its original context could violate the integrity of this system and distort the concept thus isolated. Its full meaning depended on its relation to other concepts in the Boethian system and to the system as a whole.

By including the Boethian Fortune and the Boethian providence in his narrative, Chaucer had in effect introduced a Trojan horse into his Trojan tragedy. In isolation from Boethius's system, either or both of these concepts could have heightened the tragic element in the *Troilus*, lending greater dignity to the materials of Chaucer's tragedy and clearer definition to its tragic structure. Within the Boethian system as a whole, however, the sense of human tragedy tends to dissolve into divine indifference. Tragic values lose their gravity, for the objects of earthly fear or worldly sorrow are of little weight. Tragic structure loses its clarity, for the vicissitudes of Fortune are ultimately of minor importance; moreover, adversity is actually preferable to prosperity since it may lead to a recognition of the true good. Although Boethius's emphasis on the transiency of worldly felicity might provide a valid basis for tragic poetry, the cornerstone of his system—pursuit of an otherworldly felicity based on an unchangeable good, together with contempt of the world[10] and condemnation of earthly felicity as false—would seem to undermine the traditional foundations of tragedy, shifting its emphasis from temporal to eternal values. If the goods of fortune are valueless, their loss is hardly an occasion for tragic grief. If earthly adversity and prosperity are ultimately meaningless, the fall from high degree is scarcely a breathtaking fall. The potentialities for tragedy would appear to lie less in action than in character, in the hero's ignorance of his true good, the misery of his human condition, and his bondage to passion.

If pursued to its logical conclusions, Boethian ethics might severely limit the possibilities of tragedy. If the tragic poet

---

[10] Cf. Pseudo-Aquinas, "Proemium," in *Boethius: Commentum duplex*, on the subject matter of the *Consolatio*: "Causa materialis huius libri est philosophica consolatio ordinata ad contemptum mundanorum & ad appetitum summe felicitatis." The epilogue of Chaucer's poem is similarly directed or ordered ("ordinata") toward contempt of worldly things and toward desire for the highest felicity.

accepted the doctrines of the Roman moralist, he might find the conventional tragic subjects, based as they frequently were on false conceptions of felicity and misery, inadequate for "genuine" tragedy. If he followed the philosopher and the theologian, he might run counter not only to poetic tradition but also to the feelings of the majority of his audience. If, however, he conformed to common opinions of happiness and misery, ignoring the teachings of Philosophy, he would not be describing "genuinely" tragic events. He might achieve a conventional tragedy but not (by divine standards) a true one. The only event that could be regarded as tragic in the highest sense would appear to be the loss of true beatitude.

When combined with Christian eschatological beliefs, furthermore, the Boethian *contemptus mundi* could make the conventional tragic setting seem still more inadequate. An otherworldly criterion of felicity and misery would seem to require an otherworldly setting. The truly tragic catastrophe would appear to be not so much the fall of illustrious men from high degree as the descent into Tartarus: the fall of the angels or the *Höllensturz* of the damned. The supremely tragic fate would be not so much the death of the body as that of the soul, the "second death." Shifting its emphasis from this life to the next and from this world to the world to come, a strictly Christian tragedy would find its most appropriate subject in the theme of damnation, in the vision of the Four Last Things. Substituting eternal misery for temporal adversity, it would logically hinge not so much on the loss of secular dignities as on alienation from an eternal Good.

Though Dante might pursue these arguments to their logical conclusions in the *Inferno* and the *Paradiso*, other poets, both classical and Christian, were content to seek a compromise between poetic conventions and ethical doctrines. As a tragic poet Seneca could appeal to emotions that he condemned as a Stoic philosopher, portraying calamities that he might elsewhere minimize as insignificant, evils of fortune that a Stoic might rationalize as potentially good.

Chaucer also compromises between poetic and philosophical ideas of felicity and misery. Though he follows the conventional tragic pattern based on the alternation of temporal prosperity and adversity, he is nevertheless fully aware of their final insignificance from the point of view of Boethian ethics and Christian theology. Moreover, he is equally aware that knowledge of an eternal Good is the standard whereby transitory goods and evils must be judged and condemned. His image of false felicity is incomplete without the complementary vision of true felicity. In the flight stanzas, as in the final verses of his epilogue, he places the tragic vicissitudes of his romance in their true ethical perspective, complementing the limited vision of the tragic poet with the insights of the Boethian philosopher. Faithful to the Horatian ideal of poetry as a source of moral instruction as well as pleasure, he has reoriented his poem toward the traditional end of Aristotelian and Platonic ethics and scholastic theology: the knowledge of true felicity and of the supreme Good.

The insights of Dame Philosophy tend, then, to undermine the realm of tragic values, and it is not without reason that she dismisses the Muses as "comune strompettis of swich a place that men clepen the theatre. . . ." The sufferings of the tragic hero, like those of Boethius himself, may be real, but the causes of his anguish are illusory. He suffers through his own ignorance of true and false felicity. The goods he has lost were apparent goods; the happiness from which he has fallen was a false and deceptive happiness. By definition tragedy is concerned with the theme of mutability, with the changes of Fortune, and the alternations of happiness and misery. In the context of Boethian philosophy the tragic change of state from weal to woe belongs essentially to the realm of earthly and transitory values—to *terrena* and *temporalia* —rather than to the realm of celestial truth. In this context the office of the tragic poet would appear to be essentially negative and dehortatory: to demonstrate the transiency of temporal goods and the falsity of secular bliss, to induce contempt of the world and indifference to Fortune's gifts, and (by exploiting a contrary example) to persuade his readers to seek true felicity and substantial Good elsewhere, in a realm beyond mutability and change. As a rhetorical argument the tragic *exemplum* points beyond the realm of "faithless" Fortune to the "stable faith" of the heavens, beyond the values of tragic vicissitude to a permanent and abiding felicity. The secular tragedy is incomplete; it must find its complement, and ultimately its answer, in divine comedy. Dante was the lover of Beatrice (the "divine science") not the friend of Fortune; the movement of his contemplative journey leads him from the dark wood of this world to a stable and unchanging Good. The *Commedia* concludes appropriately with a vision of the Unmoved Prime Mover and a return to the "rational motion" of the Primum Mobile. Chaucer's "tragedye" of earthly mutability similarly ends with a vision of true felicity in a stable realm beyond change. The affirmative "comic" ending complements, but does not contradict, the negative example of his tragedy.

Both Chaucer and Dante exploit the mutability-immutability *topos* to underline the antithesis between secular and celestial values, temporal and eternal goods, but in different literary genres and in different social and political contexts. Dante's quest for a continuing city, an *urbs eterna*, leads him to the City of God, to the Church Militant (the ideal of a *pax Romana* under the harmonious jurisdiction of emperor and pope) and eventually to the Church Triumphant in heaven. Chaucer's tragedy of a star-crossed lover and a fickle mistress takes place against the conventional tragic background of the transiency of secular kingdoms. The protagonist of the *Commedia*, passing from Florence to a people just and sane, finds true felicity in a divine and enduring *polis*. The hero of the *Troilus* achieves a comparable vision of beatitude, but, unlike Dante's, it is (on the surface at least) largely free of political overtones. Troilus's insights are those of the lover, not the statesman; he learns the tragic lesson of Fortune's inconstancy not from the fall of kingdoms, but through the loss of a concubine. Unaware that fate has decreed the ruin of his city, he does know that it is separating him from his mistress: "Thus to be lorn, it is my destinee." Chaucer presents the tragic theme of worldly mutability primarily in terms of the changing fortunes of a love affair. These are closely interwoven, however, with the tragic destiny of the kingdom; and the poet repeatedly reminds his audience of the national catastrophe to which the tragic hero himself is ironically deaf and blind.

Behind Dante's vision of a greater Rome and Chaucer's

romance of a Trojan lover lies another epic devoted to a Trojan hero and the destiny of Rome. In Virgil's *alta tragedia*, Dante might recognize the seeds of imperial grandeur—the planting of a Trojan colony that would eventually ripen into an eternal city, the seat of a universal empire and a universal church. Nevertheless, the *Aeneid* was also a tragedy of mutability, looking backward to the ruin of Troy and forward to the destruction of Carthage. It concerned the overthrow as well as the foundation of kingdoms. Carthage and Troy alike were subject to the rule of fate and the will of the gods. Just as the theme of Roman dominion links the *Aeneid* with the *Commedia*, the motif of the instability of kingdoms signalized by the destruction of Troy connects Virgil's "high tragedy" with Chaucer's tragic romance. In the *Troilus* the tragic theme of mutability acquires a double emphasis, from the vicissitudes of the lover and the impending ruin of the Trojan state.

If the flight stanzas undercut the tragic values of Chaucer's plot, the ultimate responsibility rests with the poet's fidelity to the Boethian system and to the Horatian ideal of the poet as moral teacher. Faced with the conflict between tragic and philosophical attitudes toward temporal prosperity and adversity, he exploits the inevitable tension between them for ironic effect. The critic should not rashly censure his "contradictions," without recognizing their origin in the poetic and ethical traditions Chaucer had inherited and without acknowledging the skill with which he attempted to combine them.

3

"What other thyng bewaylen the cryinges of tragedyes but oonly the dedes of Fortune, that with unwar strook overturneth the realmes of greet nobleye?"[11] Boethius's allusion to tragedy occurs in the midst of Dame Philosophy's apology for Fortune, and in Chaucer's translation it is followed by a gloss defining

---

[11] Boethius, Book II, prose 2; Robinson, *Works of Geoffrey Chaucer*, p. 331.

tragedy as "*a dite of prosperite for a tyme, that endeth in wrecchidnesse*," and preceded by examples of two great kings who had suffered ignominious reversals of fortune: Croesus, who had been defeated by Cyrus, and a "kyng of Percyens" who had been taken captive by Rome.[12]

Unlike the conventional tragedy, the *Troilus* centers not so much on the overthrow of realms of "great nobility" as on the misfortunes of a lover. Instead of the loss of kingdoms, Chaucer portrays the loss of a mistress. Instead of the prosperity and adversity of a monarchy, he depicts a lover's joys and sorrows. Troilus himself has little in common with Croesus or Perses; the closest analogy among the characters in the poem would have been Priam. The really tragic subject, according to Boethius's definition, would have been the fall of Troy; nevertheless, though closely linked with Troilus's fate, this does not occur within the compass of the plot. Troilus's premature death is, it would seem, a blessing in disguise; it spares him from the more tragic fate of experiencing his city's doom. In comparison with the future tragedies of other Trojans—Hecuba and Priam, Polyxena and Cassandra, Andromache and Astyanax—his calamities seem relatively light.

Except for a slight modification in structure, substituting the alternations of fortune from woe to weal to final sorrow for the conventional tragic reversal from prosperity to adversity, Chaucer has retained the traditional form of tragedy but altered its traditional content. Against the background of the tragic subject *par excellence*, the ruin of Troy, Troilus's misery must appear less miserable than it seems in his own eyes. The ironic viewpoint of the apotheosis stanzas is implicit perhaps in Chaucer's professedly "tragic" elaboration of his theme.

Finally, in addition to portraying the mutability of fortune,

---

[12] Boethius is actually referring not to a king of Persia, but to Perses, king of Macedonia, who had been defeated by Aemilius Paulus Macedonicus; see *Boethius*, trans. H. F. Stewart and E. K. Rand (London and New York, 1918), p. 180n.

tragedy aimed (in the opinion of one Boethian commentator) at the reproof of vice. According to Pseudo-Aquinas, "tragedia est carmen reprehensivum viciorum incipiens a prosperitate desinens in adversitatem." Tragic poets recount in "weeping" verse (*luctuoso carmine*) ancient exploits and the crimes of wicked kings: "antiqua gesta & facinora sceleratorum regum."[13]

Here again Chaucer's tragedy diverges significantly from the traditonal ideals of this genre. He refuses to describe his hero's gests on the battlefield, for his theme is love, not arms. Troilus is no *sceleratus*, nor is his love affair a crime (*facinus*). Though the poem may indeed be a *carmen reprehensivum*, the reproof is comparatively mild; the strongest rebuke is the hero's own condemnation of worldly vanity and the folly of those who pursue blind "lust" instead of seeking heaven.

In centering his tragedy upon the double sorrow of a lover rather than on the fall from high degree, Chaucer retained the conventional tragic emphasis on mutability but altered its content. Instead of the instability of worldly dignities, he stressed the inconstancy of earthly love. In Boethian terms both were transitory goods and could offer no more than false felicity. In the *Troilus* they occupy respectively the background and foreground of the poem. In the poet's perspective—a viewpoint that may have been consciously ironic—the loss of Criseyde dwarfs and overshadows the ruin of Troy.

---

[13] Pseudo-Aquinas on Book II, prose 2, in *Boethius: Commentum duplex*. Cf. Trivet, fol. 126: "antiqua gesta atque facinora sceleratorum regum luctuoso carmine. . . ." Defining tragedy as "carmen de magnis iniquitatibus a prosperitate incipiens & in adversitatem terminans," Trivet interprets Boethius's phrase *Quid tragoediarum clamor* as an allusion to the daily representation of fortune's mutability in the theater: "probat mutabilitatem fortune divulgari cotidianis clamoribus quia clamores poetarum cotidie in teatro recitantium tragedias nihil aliud continebant quam mutabilitatem fortune." Tragedy presents nothing other than the mutability of fortune: "Quid aliud deflet clamor tragediarum nisi fortunam vertentem regna felicia ictu indiscreto." Cf. Robertson, *A Preface to Chaucer*, pp. 346, 473, on the definitions of tragedy by Trivet and Radulphus de Longo Campo.

Instead of emphasizing the felicity of a kingdom, Chaucer has stressed the delights of the flesh, and the "tragic" action of his poem turns accordingly not so much on the hero's attainment and loss of a realm as on his winning and losing a mistress. Criseyde's physical presence or absence, and her fidelity or infidelity to her lover, occupy a central position not only in the structure of the plot but also in the framework of Boethian doctrine underlying the entire poem. According to Pseudo-Aquinas, a man should be indifferent to all temporal and transitory goods, neither grieving at their absence nor rejoicing in their presence. Since they cannot offer true felicity, they do not merit either grief or joy: ". . . ostendit bona temporalia esse transitoria et non consistere totaliter in eius [*sic*] totalem veram felicitatem. & per consequens non esse dolendum de eorum absentia: nec gaudendum de eorum presentia. et neminem debere extolli in prosperis: nec deprimi in adversis."[14] The poles upon which Chaucer's tragic fable turns are inevitably negated by the Boethian values he has introduced into his poem. In the eyes of Dame Philosophy the possession and loss of Criseyde would have offered no valid cause for either joy or grief.

4

Throughout the greater part of the *Troilus*, the hero's predicament is roughly analogous to that of Boethius in the opening books of the *Consolation*. It is not until the end that he learns, through his experience of a faithless mistress, what Boethius (with the aid of Dame Philosophy) has learned through experience of faithless Fortune: the instability of temporal goods. If Chaucer gives definitive expression to this concept in the epilogue, he has nevertheless implied it throughout the poem. Against the background of Boethian commentary, the analogy between Criseyde's inconstancy and the inconstancy of Fortune must appear deliberate.

Commenting on Boethius's condemnation of Fortune as "faith-

---

[14] Pseudo-Aquinas, "Proemium," in *Boethius: Commentum duplex*.

less," Pseudo-Aquinas amplifies this *topos* with quotations from Seneca:[15]

. . . appellat fortunam malefidam: quia est deceptiva. . . . Unde Sene[ca]. Neminem adversa fortuna comminuit nisi quem fecunda [secunda] decipit. Et alibi Sene[ca]. Fortuna nemini servat fidem: nulli obesse semel contenta est: quem nimium fovet hunc stultum facit . . . fortune bona dicuntur levia: quia transitoria. Non enim perdurat circa hominem. . . .

The same author also emphasizes woman's inconstancy: "etiam si bonam uxorem habuisti non potes affirmare eam esse permansuram in illo proposito: nihil tam mobile nihil tam vagum quam feminarum voluntas."[16] To medieval and Renaissance writers alike, Virgil's dictum *varium et mutabile semper Femina* (*Aeneid*, IV, 569) seemed axiomatic, and, in one form or another, this concept entered rhetorical manuals and treatises on poetics as an aspect of the decorum of persons. In his *Ars versificatoria* Matthieu de Vendôme cited Virgil's lines as an example of personal attributes (*attributa personae*) according to nature; in this passage he finds an *argumentum* or *locus* according to sex.[17] The same tradition survives in Renaissance poetics. According to Ascensius, women are by nature inconstant and prone to deceit, and the poet must bear these qualities in mind in order to observe *decorum personarum*:[18]

Decorum sexum afflagitat ut longe alia sint que viris attribuuntur quam que feminis . . . femine enim sunt inconstantes. modo nimium blande & affabiles. modo minaces aspere & proterve. modo iocose. modo tristes. modo amice. modo inimice. Sed status & genus vite in primis advertendum est. Viri autem constantiores & prudentiores ut plurimum sunt: quamvis feminis non desit solertia: & ad fallendum calliditas.

In contrasting Criseyde's inconstancy with Troilus's constancy,

---

[15] Pseudo-Aquinas on Book I, meter 1, in *ibid*. Trivet, fol. 107, explains that fortune (".s. temporalium mutabilitas") is called "male fida" because a man can ill confide or trust ("male . . . confidere") in her favors.

[16] Pseudo-Aquinas on Book II, prose 4, in *Boethius: Commentum duplex*.

[17] Edmond Faral, ed., *Les arts poétiques du XIIe et du XIIIe siècle* (Paris, 1958), pp. 136-137.

[18] Iodocus Badius Ascensius, "Proemium," in *Boethius: Commentum duplex*.

Chaucer has not merely observed decorum in character but has developed this antithesis in Boethian terms as an argument against placing one's trust in a temporal, and therefore transitory, good. In treating the lovers' affections—another aspect of *decorum personarum*—he not only observes "congruity" in *affectiones* and decorum in age (youth being prone to love, manhood to the pursuit of honors and riches, and old age to avarice), but he is also conscious of the values of Boethian ethics, which regarded all passions directed toward temporal objects as injurious. Defining affection as a movement involving the senses and imagination and obstructing right reason ("affectio est motus particule sensitive sub fantasia boni vel mali animum afficiens et rectum rationis iudicium impediens"), Pseudo-Aquinas distinguishes four principal emotions under which all others can be reduced.[19] These are joy, hope, fear, and sorrow (*gaudium, spes, timor, et dolor*). Each of these passions is twofold, insofar as it is directed to a present or to an absent good or evil. Whereas joy concerns a present and hope a future good, grief is directed toward a present and fear toward a future evil. Though potentially virtuous if ordered toward their proper ends, all these passions are injurious when directed toward earthly objects.

Chaucer has dwelt at length on Criseyde's characteristic inclination to fear, on Troilus's alternations between hope and despair and his interlude of joy in the midst of his double sorrow, and on Pandarus's sympathetic involvement in the emotions of the lovers. Without exception, these various passions are all directed toward earthly objects, transitory goods or evils. From the Boethian viewpoint of the epilogue they must stand condemned as harmful. Though the poet may communicate his own sympathy for his characters caught in their tangled labyrinth of affections, though he may engage the emotions of his readers, his final censure should come as no surprise. In the Boethian context of his story, his rejection is not inconsistent, but inevitable.

When Troilus condemns the vanity and ignorance of those who neglect the heavens for blind and transitory "lust," he is

---

[19] Pseudo-Aquinas on Book I, meter 7, in *ibid*.

echoing a Boethian commonplace. Dame Philosophy had reprov-
ed Boethius in similar terms, and the repetition of this commonplace underscores the analogy between Troilus's despair and
Boethius's grief. Different as they are, both men have been
blinded by emotion, by concern for temporal things, and by the
power of sensuality. In commenting on the opening passages of
the *Consolation*, Pseudo-Aquinas interprets the dialogue between
Boethius and Philosophy as an inner debate between passion and
reason:[20] "Boetius dolens & ipsa philosophia ipsum consolans non
sunt aliud nisi animus dolens ex oppressione sensualitatis: & ratio
consolans ex vigore sapientie." Unlike the *Consolation*, the *Troilus*
does not personify philosophy; a comparable debate between
reason and sensuality occurs, however, in Troilus's soliloquy in
Book IV.

In Philosophy's first reply (*Heu quam precipiti mersa profundo*), the commentator finds a double application: first, to
humanity in general; and second, to Boethius himself: "Primo
universaliter philosophia deplangit perturbationem mentis hominum. Secundo spetialiter convertit planctum super boe. ibi." The
burden of her complaint is that, sunk in temporal cares, mankind
neglects the light of contemplation, follows sense and lust instead
of reason, and neglects the knowledge of its Creator for external
goods and sensual delights: [21]

Heu quam .i. quantum mens hominum hebet .i. obscuratur mersa
precipiti profundo id est cura rerum temporalium que precipitant
hominem: & talis mens relicta propria luce .i. contemplatione tendit .i.
laborat ire in tenebras externas .i. in ignorantias exteriores. . . . Nota

---

[20] Pseudo-Aquinas on Book I, prose 1, in *ibid*.

[21] Pseudo-Aquinas on Book I, meter 2 in *ibid*. Trivet's commentary (fol.
109) similarly develops the contrast between Boethius's solicitude for temporal
things and his former contemplation of the heavens, free of temporal care.
Commenting on the phrase *Heu quam precipiti mersa profundo*, he explains
cura as "sollicitudo temporalium" and *profundo* as an allusion to the
"sollicitudine rerum temporalium qua homo ab altitudine dignitatis precipitatur
ad ea quae sub se sunt. . . ." Formerly, when Boethius had contemplated the
heavens, he had been free from care for temporal things: "solutus a cura
temporalium *celo aperto* .s. per agnitionem quod clauditur per ignoranciam
suetus .i. assuetus *ire* .s. motu rationis . . . *in ethereos meatus*. . . ."

quod in nobis est duplex virtus. rationalis & sensualis. sensus autem semper adversatur rationi: quia caro concupiscit adversus spiritum: & spiritus adversus carnem. Cum autem sensualitas vincit rationem: tunc homo est in malo statu regiminis & efficitur bestialis. . . . Valde conandum & laborandum est nobis ut virtus nostra concupiscibilis subiecta fit rationi. . . . Plures autem homines sequuntur sensualitatem quam rationem: insudantes bonis exterioribus & delectationibus sensualibus: per que impediuntur in speculatione & cognitione summi boni: . . . Item cum anima ingerit se curis rerum temporalium profunde precipitatur & hebet: quia a cognitione rerum & sui creatoris destituitur: & destituta cadit in tenebras externas .i. in ignorantias exteriores.

From this general censure of mankind, Philosophy now turns to Boethius himself, who has turned from the contemplation of the heavens—from astronomy, natural philosophy, and metaphysics—to earthly affairs: ". . . destitutus a tali contemplatione solum de terrenis cogitabat." Bearing the heavy chains of the passions ("gravidis cathenis passionum") and bowed down by the weight of temporal losses ("pondere amissionis rerum temporalium"), he has fixed his mind on earthly goods ("bona terrena que homines stolidos efficiunt"). Just as a chain detains a creature contrary to its nature, Pseudo-Aquinas continues, the four affections detain man's soul, drawing it toward forbidden objects contrary to its nature and to reason, which naturally desires the best: "Nam ratio semper deprecatur ad optima."

To his interpretation of Boethius's verses, Pseudo-Aquinas brought his knowledge of Seneca and Saint Albertus Magnus, of Aristotle's *Ethics* ("in antiqua translatione"), and even of Hermes Trismegistus. Quoting Scripture on the lust of the flesh against the spirit (Gal. 5:17), he reduced Boethius's inner conflict to the struggle of sensuality against reason. Though Chaucer could hardly expect the same range of classical and Christian erudition on the part of his wider audience, he might expect it from a few judicious readers such as "moral Gower" and the "philosophical Strode." To these, Troilus's anguish might be subject to the same reproaches that Dame Philosophy had leveled against Boethius and against the generality of mankind; it proceeds from *cura* or *sollicitudo rerum temporalium*. In Chaucer's "woful" verses on Troilus's "double sorwe" they might perceive, beneath the poet's expressed sympathy for the protagonist's sufferings, a lament that (like Dame Philosophy's verses) implies rebuke. Like Philosophy's *planctus*, Chaucer's "tragedye"—his *carmen luctuosum*—might seem a lament for the tyranny of blind passion; like Philosophy, he too bewails the passion of the mind: "deplangit perturbationem mentis hominum." Like other tragedies, the *Troilus* might appear to be a *carmen reprehensivum viciorum*, even though the vices it portrays are more amiable than those of the conventional tragic protagonist and spring rather from concupiscence than from violence or fraud. For such readers the Boethian commonplaces of the epilogue would be consistent with the Boethian concepts expressed throughout the poem; and the fundamental antitheses of the epilogue—the opposition between earthly inconstancy and eternal stability, between love of the creature and love of the Creator, and between worldly and heavenly felicity—would seem not only "congruous" and probable, but necessary. They are precisely the sort of commentary that Strode and Gower might have expected.

5

Though Chaucer has retained the conventional structure of tragedy, he has replaced its traditional subject matter with an erotic content; instead of the fall of kings, he portrays the misfortunes of a lover. In his treatment of Boethian themes, we may detect a similar shift of emphasis. Though he retains the conventional Boethian attitude toward solicitude for temporal things ("cura rerum temporalium"), he focuses his attention primarily on the cares of the lover.[22] This in itself was hardly

---

[22] For the use of the term *care* (or *cares*) to designate the sorrows and anxieties of the lover, cf. *Troilus*, Book I, lines 505, 550 587; IV, 579. In Chaucer's account of how Troilus lies "Ibounden in the blake bark of care, Disposed wood out of his wit to breyde" (IV, 229-230), there may be a concrete allusion to the melancholy basis of the lover's malady. Cf. also the references to "colde care" (I, 612) and "cares colde" (I, 264; III, 1202, 1260; IV, 1690; V, 1342, 1347). Chaucer also employs the terms *cure* and *business* as equivalents of the Latin *cura*. Thus Criseyde (III, 1041-1042) diagnoses

surprising; he was, after all, writing a love story, not a commentary on the *De Consolatione*. Nevertheless, in the context of an erotic romance, the solicitude of a lover could acquire shades of meaning belonging primarily to medical rather than to Boethian tradition. It was an essential feature of heroic love, that *amor nobilis* which medieval and Renaissance physicians classified among diseases of the head and which, left unchecked or uncured, might end in insanity or death. According to Burton,[23] "Avicenna . . . calleth this passion *ilishi*, and defines it, *to be a disease or melancholy vexation, or anguish of minde; in which a man continually meditates of the beauty, gestures, manners, of his mistris, and troubles himself about it. . . .*" In the Latin translation of Avicenna's treatise, *ilishi* is explicitly defined as "melancholy solicitude": "Haec aegritudo est solicitudo melancholica, in quâ homo applicat sibi continuam cogitationem super pulchritudine ipsius quam amat, gestuum, morum."[24]

Similar definitions occur in other medical treatises. As Professor Robertson has noted,[25] Bernardus de Gordonio followed Avicenna's opinion, defining *hereos* as "sollicitudo melancolica

---

Troilus's supposed jealousy as naught "but illusioun, Of habundaunce of love and besy cure, That doth youre herte this disese endure"; and elsewhere (IV, 1645) she complains that Love is full of "bisy drede." In the Knight's Tale (line 1928) Bisynesse and Jalousye are depicted, among other allegorical figures, on the walls of Venus' temple; earlier in the same poem (line 1007) Chaucer associates "bisyness and cure," though in reference to the diligence of "pilours" on the Theban battlefield rather than to the anxiety of lovers. In his translation of the *Consolation of Philosophy*, he renders Boethius's *cura* (Book I, meter 2) as "anoyos bysynes"; cf. also "the pleyinge bysynes of men" (Book III, meter 2), "bytynge bysynesse" (Book III, meter 3), "bytynges of bysynesse" (Book III, prose 5).

[23] Robert Burton, *The Anatomy of Melancholy* (London, 1837), II, 207-208.

[24] Burton, II, 207; c.f. *Liber Avicenne* (Venice, 1500, HEH # 100359), Book III, tractatus 4, chap. 24.

[25] Robertson, *A Preface to Chaucer*, pp. 109-110, 458; cf. Bernardus de Gordonio, *Practica sive Lilium medicinae* (Venice, 1498, HEH # 87627), particula II, chap. 20. Cf. John Livingston Lowes, "The Loveres Maladye of Hereos," *MP*, XI (1914), 491-546.

propter mulieris amorem. . . . Et quia [philocaptus] est in continua meditatione: ideo sollicitudo melancolica appellatur." Similarly, in his *Practica medicinae* Giovanni Michele Savonarola[26] defined *ilishi* as "sollicitudo melancolica qua quis ob amorem fortem & intensum sollicitat habere rem quam nimia aviditate concupiscit: . . . Dicitur sollicitudo quia tales facti iam melancolici ex amore inordinato sunt in continua cogitatione memoria & imaginatione: ita ut non dormiant neque bibant. . . ."

In English poetry, as in Continental literature, this idea left a long and distinguished record, ranging from "the loveris maladye of Hereos" in Chaucer's Knight's Tale to Spenser's account of Scudamour's ordeal in the House of Care. In the *Troilus* this concept acquires Boethian connotations in addition to its original medical significance. In the hero's double sorrows we may recognize not only the *cura* for which Philosophy reproaches Boethius—the *cura rerum temporalium* of Pseudo-Aquinas and the *insensata cura de' mortali* of Dante—but also (more specifically) the *solicitudo melancholica* of Avicenna and his successors. Like Boethius, Troilus has fallen into "a commune seknesse to hertes that been deceyved"; but, unlike Boethius, he lacks the nourishing "medicyne" of Philosophy.

Like the commentators on Boethius's *affectio*, medical discussions of *hereos* emphasize the subordination of reason to imagination, the corruption of rational judgment, and the combination of a false conception of felicity with passionate desire for a false or transitory good. Just as Boethian tradition had stressed the illusory nature of every joy based on temporary and secular good, medical tradition had emphasized the lover's mistaken belief that the enjoyment of his mistress's beauty constituted the highest felicity. For Bernardus (as Professor Robertson points out),[27] *hereos* resulted from the corruption of the "estima-

---

[26] Giovanni Michele Savonarola, *Practica medicinae* (Venice, 1497, HEH # 95857), tractatus VI, chap. 14.

[27] Robertson, *A Preface to Chaucer*, pp. 49, 458-459; cf. Bernardus, particula II, chap. 20; Burton, *Anatomy*, I, 155, "*Phantasie*, or imagination, which some call *aestimative*, or *cogitative*. . . ."

tive" virtue ("Corruptio extimative propter formam et figuram fortiter affixam"); ardently desiring his beloved, the lover regards her as his end and his felicity; "unde cum aliquis philocaptus est in amore alicuius mulieris: ita fortiter concipit formam et figuram ad modum . . . et ideo ardenter concupiscit eam: et sine modo & mensura opinans si posset finem attingere: quae hec esset sua felicitas et beatitudo: & intantum corruptum est iuditium rationis. . . ." Again, "sicut felicitas est ultimum dilectionis: ita hereos ultimum dilectionis. & ideo intantum concupiscunt quod insani efficiuntur."

Both Bernardus and Savonarola (1384-1461) give detailed accounts of the physiological and psychological aspects of *hereos*; and, like Bernardus, Savonarola attributes its cause to the corruption of the "estimative virtue." According to the latter's treatis, "Coniuncta autem est nimia & continua operatio virtutis imaginative & cogitative circa desiderium rei comprehense. Et modus generationis est quia apprehenso obiecto a virtute imaginativa primo per sensum exteriorem sibi deportato secundum plurimum tamquam multum delectabili: deinde virtus extimativa inducit ipsum esse appetendum & ultra quam conveniat. & in hoc corrumpitur iudicium. . . . Existimativa quae est virtus altior imperat deinde imaginative. & imaginativa concupiscibili: & concupiscibile irascibili: & irascibile motive lacertorum. et sic totum corpus movetur spreto ordine rationis & discutit de nocte & die vagando spernendo frigus. calores. pericula & huiusmodi stans in continua cogitatione & concupiscentia ad rem desideratam. . . ."

Because the lover's judgment has been corrupted by imagination and sense (Savonarola explains), he overestimates the true worth of his beloved. To possess her seems, in his mistaken judgment, to be his true felicity: "unde filocapti super omnem rem amasiam appetunt omnia alia spernentes & existimantes suam felicitatem esse si habere possent. & sic de his quae talia sine usu rationis appetunt." Just as the Boethian commentators stress the transiency of all worldly goods, Savonarola emphasizes the transiency of the lover's delight: "O miseri qui ex tam parva ac cito transitoria delectatione tam gravia & quasi insupportabilia ut

sunt non timere frigus neque vigilias continuas. sitim: famem &
huiusmodi videntur facilia & delectabilia. ut ribaldones qui vitio
ludi aut vini nudi incedunt."[28]

By introducing *hereos* into a Boethian frame of reference,
Chaucer subjected the lover's solicitude to Philosophy's sweeping
condemnation of temporal cares. Combining medical and ethical
tradition, he brought together two highly specialized conceptions
of solicitude and two conventional ideas of false felicity. Both
traditions had stressed the distortion of rational judgment by
passion. Both had regarded the lover's delights as transitory and
his opinion of felicity as irrational. In the epilogue, Chaucer
depicts the lover's return to right reason and rational judgment.
After portraying a mistaken notion of felicity and a false opinion
of the chief good, Chaucer brings his hero to a vision of eternal
stability and knowledge of "pleyn felicity." Troilus's ascent to the
eighth sphere is not only a progression from an imaginary
heaven—an earthly paradise that cannot endure—to the real
heavens but also a "rational movement" from creature to Creator. It is as much a recovery of his "estimative virtue" as a
reorientation of his will. Boethius had been free "to gon in
hevenliche pathes" *per rationem* and to contemplate the "wandrynge recourses" of each *stella erratica* only insofar as he had
been free from solicitude for temporal things, "solutus a cura
rerum temporalium."[29] Released from the body and its appetites,
Troilus is likewise free to contemplate the "erratik sterres" and to
"herken" their "armonye." Like Boethius's astronomical meditations, Troilus's intellectual vision is closely associated wth release
from the malady of temporal cares, but in his case the disease is
more easily diagnosed. It is *Ilishi* or *Hereos*, the solicitude of the
lover.

Thus far the flight stanzas have been examined in their
relation to the Boethian framework of Chaucer's *tragedye* and the

---

[28] Savonarola, tractatus VI, chap. 14.

[29] Cf. Pseudo-Aquinas on Book I, meter 2 in *Boethius: Commentum
duplex.*

significance of Boethian values for his treatment of plot, character, and passion. In the final chapters, consideration will be given to this passage in a narrower context, in its immediate relationship to the verses on Troilus's death.

CHAPTER VI

THE REVISED EPILOGUE:
THEMATIC PATTERNS

The flight stanzas are the last, and perhaps the most striking, of Chaucer's major additions to Boccaccio's epilogue. In the earlier version of the *Troilus*, as in the *Filostrato*, the poet's reflections on the hero's end had followed immediately after the terse and unembellished summary of his death:[1]

>. . .e dopo lungo stallo,
>Avendone già morti più di mille,
>Miseramente un dì l' uccise Achille.
>
>But, weilawey, save only goddes wille!
>Ful pitously hym slough the fierse Achille.

This is the "wretched end" that medieval definitions of tragedy might have led the reader to expect, and both poets immediately turn to its tragic implications. For Boccaccio, this was the end of Troilus's hopes and tribulations as a lover, the premature end of abilities that might have graced a royal throne:

>Cotal fine ebbe il mal concetto amore
>Di Troilo in Criseida, e cotale
>Fin' ebbe il miserabile dolore
>Di lui, al qual non fu mai altro eguale;
>Cotal fin' ebbe il lucido splendore
>Che lui servava al solìo reale;
>Cotal fin' ebbe la speranza vana
>Di Troilo in Criseida villana.

Like Boccaccio, Chaucer utilizes a figure of repetition (*cotal fine, swich fyn*) to emphasize the wretched end of his protagonist, but he nevertheless alters both the content and structure of this passage. Omitting the allusions to Troilus's "miserable grief" and "vain hope" and the pejorative adjectives *mal concetto* and

---

[1] *The Filostrato of Giovanni Boccaccio*, trans. Nathaniel Edward Griffin and Arthur Beckwith Myrick (Philadelphia, 1929), p. 496; Robert Kilburn Root, *The Book of Troilus and Cryseyde* (Princeton, 1926), p. 402.

villana, he retains the references to *amore* and to royal station but places them in a new context heavily weighted with Boethian commonplaces. As Dame Philosophy had warned her disciple, worldly dignities, royal estate, earthly pleasures, and secular nobility are transitory goods and cannot offer true happiness. After this catalogue of Boethian examples of false felicity, Chaucer concludes his argument with a generalization equally Boethian ("Swych fyn hath false worldes brotelnesse!") and finishes his stanza with a brief summary of the content of his narrative:

> Swich fyn hath, lo, this Troilus for love!
> Swich fyn hath al his grete worthynesse!
> Swich fyn hath his estat real above!
> Swich fyn his lust! swich fyn hath his noblesse!
> Swich fyn hath false worldes brotelnesse!
> And thus bigan his lovyng of Criseyde,
> As I have told, and in this wise he deyde.

In the five stanzas following these reflections on Troilus's end, the divergences between the two poems in theme and structure are even more pronounced. Though each poet begins with a direct appeal to his youthful audience:

> O giovanetti, ne' quai coll' etate
> Surgendo vien l' amoroso disio, . . .

> O yonge fresshe folkes, he or she,
> In which that love up groweth with youre age, . . .

the resemblances cease after this initial apostrophe. Where Boccaccio emphasizes woman's inconstancy, Chaucer stresses the transiency of the world. Where Boccaccio addresses his admonition exclusively to young men, Chaucer includes women also among his audience of "yonge . . . folkes." Where Boccaccio directs all five stanzas to youthful lovers, Chaucer addresses his penultimate stanza to more learned characters ("moral Gower" and "philosophical Strode") and directs his final stanza to the Trinity.

Rhetorically, both poets attempt to dissuade as well as persuade, but in Boccaccio's epilogue dehortatory arguments tend to predominate. Urging his youthful hearers to profit by Troilus's example lest they meet a similar fate, he advises them to restrain

"I pronti passi all' appetito rio" and to be cautious in trusting all women ("Non di leggieri a tutte crederete"). In words that recall Virgil's dictum and anticipate the aria of Verdi's profligate duke, he reminds them that "Giovane donna è mobile." A young woman is proud of her beauty, inclined to many lovers, and as fickle as a leaf in the wind: "Volubil sempre come foglia al vento." A noblewoman is apt to be haughty and disdainful, and an older woman may not be much the wiser for her years. Though one should search for a perfect lady ("perfetta donna") who will keep her promises, one should not choose in haste.

Finally, after asking compassion for his hero, the poet bids his youthful audience to invoke Love on Troilus's behalf and to pray that they themselves may love shrewdly instead of dying because of an evil woman:

> Conceda grazia si d' amare accorti,
> Che per ria donna alfin non siate morti.

Having ended this section of his poem with a plea for judicious restraint but without a single allusion to the dichotomy of earthly and heavenly love or to the mutability of all worldly goods, Boccaccio proceeds to the final section of his poem; this is devoted entirely to a farewell to his book.

In contrast with Boccaccio's appeal, Chaucer's address to the young folk is otherworldly rather than mundane, and predominantly hortatory rather than dissuasive. In the previous stanza on Troilus's end, he had already shifted the emphasis from Criseyde's inconstancy to the mutability of all earthly felicity. Instead of condemning "Criseida villana," he meditates on the brittleness of *all* worldly joys: "Swych fyn hath false worldes brotelnesse!" This in itself is essentially a negative argument, based on the conventional *contemptus mundi*, and in the following stanzas he amplifies it by similar dehortations from "worldly vanyte" and from "This world, that passeth soone as floures faire." At the same time, however, he complements these dehortatory appeals with positive exhortations to the true Good:

> Repeyreth hom fro worldly vanyte,
> And of youre herte up casteth the visage
> To thilke god that after his ymage

Yow made. . . .
For he nyl falsen no wight, dar I seye,
That wol his herte al holly on hym leye.
And syn he best to love is, and most meke,
What nedeth feyned loves for to seke?

Like Boccaccio, Chaucer has taken the example of Criseyde's faithlessness as his point of departure, but he exploits it for very different lines of argument. Where Boccaccio had stressed the fickleness of young women, Chaucer emphasizes the fickleness of the world. Though both poets had employed arguments from comparison or contrast, Boccaccio had utilized such arguments to demonstrate the difficulty of finding a perfect mistress; Chaucer, to prove the superiority of divine love. The contrary to Criseyde's faithlessness—which, unlike Boccaccio, Chaucer does not explicitly mention after Stanza 254—is not simply a mistress who will keep her promises; it is God himself, who "nyl falsen no wight." In these lines the poet has given Boethius's "stable feyth" a Christian reference, and he will subsequently underline this point by his allusion to "that sothfast Crist" in his apostrophe to Gower and Strode.

The third stanza (265) in this passage ("Lo here, of payens corsed olde rites!") has no parallel in the *Filostrato*. It is Chaucer's own addition to the epilogue. Amplifying and complementing the earlier meditation on Troilus's end (stanza 262) and the exhortation to the young folk (263-264) to repair "hom fro worldly vanyte" and return to the true God, it stresses the futility of "thise wrecched worldes appetites" and the "fyn and guerdoun for travaille" in the service of the false gods of the Gentiles. At the same time it undercuts the literary tradition of antiquity:

> Lo here, the forme of old clerkes speche
> In poetrie, if ye hire bokes seche!

Like Troilus's brittle joys and the appetites of this world, the religion and literature of the ancients have been the victims of time and change. Chaucer's own verse, as he is well aware, may also be subject to corruption (stanza 257), and perhaps in this context we should interpret the reference to "feyned loves" (line 1848) in a literary as well as an ethical sense, not only as an allusion to the deceits of earthly lovers and the falseness of worldly lust in comparison with heavenly love but also as a reference to the erotic fictions of the poets, to the literary imitation of "thise wrecched worldes appetites," and to poetic exploitation of the cult of Venus and Amor and the machinery of the pagan gods.

Stanzas 262 and 265 are linked by the *fyn-topos* (lines 1828, 1852), by the same rhetorical device (repetition of the initial phrases "Swich fyn" and "Lo here"), and by the common theme of mutability. Both stress the ultimate vanity of earthly goods and worldly appetites—the inevitable end that awaits the values of the "false" and "wrecched" world; and both stand in striking contrast to stanzas 263 and 264 and the two concluding stanzas, with their emphasis on the stability and immutability of the supreme Good.

Such was the narrative and thematic context into which Chaucer inserted the flight stanzas, appropriately grafting this cutting from Boccaccio's *Teseida* between two lines from the *Filostrato*. Aside from these, Boccaccio's influence in the final portion of the epilogue is slight. His stanza on the end of Troilo's "mal concetto amore" had been converted into a Boethian meditation on *contemptus mundi*, and his worldly advice to practical lovers transformed into a Christian exhortation to divine love. The essential insights of the flight passage were already inherent in the unrevised epilogue, just as the values of the epilogue had been implicit (and not infrequently explicit) in the Boethian commonplaces that pervade the narrative itself.

1

From the Boethian and Christian *topoi* of the final stanzas let us return briefly to the earlier portions of the epilogue and review their narrative and thematic context. In this case also it will be helpful to summarize some of the principal similarities and dissimilarities between Chaucer's poem and Boccaccio's.

In both poems the story of Troilus and Criseyde had virtually ended with the final dialogue between Troilus and Pandarus. The latter's speech (stanzas 248-249 in Chaucer; nos. 23-24 in

Boccaccio) expressing his distress and declaring that he had sacrificed "mio onore" for "tuo amore" is the last instance of direct discourse among any of the characters in the poem. From this point on, both poets drop the dramatic mode entirely for a brief summary of the remaining action and for moral reflections.

The next two stanzas in the *Filostrato* (25-26) summarize the triangular relationship between the three lovers, reporting Troilus's fruitless clashes with Diomede and stressing the role of Fortune in thwarting both love and revenge. Chaucer has expanded Boccaccio's account so that it now covers three stanzas instead of two, amplifying the first with a moral reflection on the way of the world: "In ech estat is litel hertes reste." Immediately after these stanzas (250-252) follow five stanzas apparently original with Chaucer. In the first he excuses himself for not reporting Troilus's battles in detail; his theme has been the love, rather than "The armes of this ilke worthi man"; for "His worthi dedes" one should consult Dares. The next two stanzas (254-255) are addressed to the gentlewomen in his audience, apologizing for portraying an unfaithful woman, and the following stanzas (256-257) bid farewell to his book. With the next stanza (258) he returns to Boccaccio's account of Troilo's "Ira . . . in tempi diversi" (27) and his death at the hands of Achilles.

The author's apology to the ladies does not occur in the *Filostrato*, and Chaucer's *envoi* differs both in content and in position from Boccaccio's. In at least one respect their position is somewhat anomalous. Chaucer places them *before* the account of Troilus's death, separating them from the concluding addresses to the "yonge fresshe folkes," to Gower and Strode, and to the Trinity. Thematically, however, they are related to the final stanzas of the epilogue and indirectly to the flight passage. Moreover, by taking up the inevitable topic of infidelity at this point, Chaucer is able to shift his emphasis later (unlike Boccaccio) from Criseyde's faithlessness to the world's inconstancy and the "sothfast" faith of the Creator.

The theme of Troilus's love (stanza 253) leads, not illogically, to that of Criseyde's infidelity in the following verses. Judiciously forestalling possible criticism by following up his narrative of Criseyde's "gilt"—so bitterly lamented by her lover and so savagely denounced by her uncle—with an apology *in propria persona*, he converts this unfavorable example into a topic for flattery. To the single example of a faithless mistress he opposes two instances of faithful wives and concludes by shifting the stigma of treason from women to men. Nevertheless, infidelity remains the principal theme of both stanzas, and paradoxically the poet's argument *ad feminam* gives it greater prominence. By apologizing for Criseyde's "gilt," Chaucer has in effect added his own accusation to those of Troilus and Pandarus. Moreover, following the rhetorical axiom that an idea is defined more clearly through juxtaposition with its contrary, he brings her guilt into sharper focus through contrast with its opposite virtue: the faithfulness of Penelope and "good Alceste." Finally, he gives further emphasis to the theme of the lover's unfaithfulness by broadening its reference, extending its application from women to men. The net effect of this passage is to underline the motif of inconstancy and indirectly to heighten our awareness of Troilus's exemplary fidelity through comparison with the faithlessness of other men. Chaucer's final warning to the ladies ("Beth war of men") is couched in universal terms.

In thus taking Criseyde's guilt as its point of departure for developing the antithesis between fidelity and infidelity, Chaucer's apology serves a proleptic as well as a retrospective function. Drawing a universal inference from the particular story recounted in this *tragedye*, it announces a theme that will receive fuller expression in the six final stanzas of the epilogue, in the contrast between true and false love, steadfastness and mutability. The flight episode would eventually give concrete expression to similar themes.

From the gentlewomen Chaucer turns to his book, taking leave of his manuscript before bidding farewell to his hero or to his audience. Here again one encounters the theme of mutability, albeit in a different form. Aware of the vicissitudes and transiency of the spoken and the written word, the poet prays "that non myswrite the, Ne the mysmetre for defaute of tonge." A similar *topos* will occur later, near the very end of the epilogue:

> Lo here, the forme of olde clerkes speche
> In poetrie, if ye hire bokes seche!

Both these passages serve a proleptic function, even though this is not their primary purpose nor their ostensible intent. Both obliquely announce a theme that will receive clearer and more forceful expression in Chaucer's reflections on "false worldes brotelnesse" and "worldly vanyte" in the latter stanzas of the original epilogue and ultimately in the insights of the flight passage, with its condemnation of the wretched world and its transitory lust.

2

Though the flight passage belonged originally to the *Teseida*, Chaucer evidently regarded it as more appropriate for the tragedy of Troilus than for the story of Arcita. One of the principal considerations prompting his decision may have been the strongly Boethian (and Christian) content of his epilogue. An additional factor may have been narrative context: the different circumstances surrounding Troilus's death and that of Arcita. By examining the immediate context of the hero's death in the *Troilus* and the Knight's Tale, we may achieve a clearer understanding of the literary strategy behind Chaucer's variations on his sources.

In both these episodes Chaucer reversed Boccaccio's treatment of the hero's death. Though Boccaccio had devoted three stanzas to Arcita's flight into the heavens, he had said little about Troilo's destination. Instead he had urged his audience to pray to Love for the peace of Troilo's soul:

> . . . ed orazione
> Per lui fate ad amor pietosamente,
> Ch' el posi in pace in quella regione
> Dov' el dimora, . . .

Chaucer, however, devoted the same three stanzas to Troilus, but explicitly disavowed any knowledge of Arcita's whereabouts. Boccaccio had been entirely preoccupied with Troilo's earthly fate and with the worldly lesson his *giovanetti* might learn from this example. From the account of Troilo's miserable death he had passed directly to his reflections on the consequences of the hero's ill-conceived love for Criseida.

Chaucer's indebtedness to the *Teseida* for his flight stanzas may overshadow the minor but significant changes he made in adapting them to a different literary context: a different poem with a different hero, a different heroine, and a different kind of love affair. In the *Troilus* they are closely related, thematically and structurally, with the rest of the epilogue. In the *Teseida* they occur at the beginning of the penultimate book, and a substantial amount of funeral and nuptial pageantry will intervene before the narrative reaches its end.

Despite occasional diatribes against this passage as an in-artistic blunder, most readers will probably applaud Chaucer's literary tact in transferring it from the story of Arcita and Emilia to that of Troilus and Criseyde. Though in both poems its immediate context is (necessarily) the hero's death, there are nevertheless significant differences in circumstances. Boccaccio's Arcita dies with his lady's name on his lips, calling on her whom he had loved most in the world. An instant later, before the syllables of her name have quite faded away, we hear him damning the vain endeavors of those who pursue the world's false beauty. He himself was among these, and the use of the term *falsa biltate* and the repetition of the word *mondo* underline the fact that he is denouncing his own love affair. So sudden a *volteface* might seem praiseworthy to a Stoic philosopher (and a theologian might hail it as a deathbed conversion!), but by chivalric standards it comes perilously close to *villania*. It is churlish behavior—bad manners, if not infidelity. Whereas Pompey's laughter at *sui ludibria trunci* emphasizes his magnanimity and thus heightens heroic decorum, Arcita's derision violates the decorum of a noble and courteous lover. Chaucer did well (one feels) to exclude this passage from the Knight's Tale and to disavow any authoritative knowledge as to the destination of Arcite's soul.

In the *Troilus*, however, the immediate context is different. The hero is not taking leave of a newly won bride; moreover, in contrast to Emelye, his Criseyde has been egregiously faithless. Nor has he died uttering his lady's name either in blessing or in curse. The immediate context of the flight passage is the account of his "pitous" death and the reflections on his wretched end; the latter (as we have seen) had already undergone extensive transformation in Chaucer's hands. In adapting Boccaccio's stanza on Arcita's *fine*, he had replaced the overt censure of Criseyde with examples of false felicity derived from the third book of the *Consolation of Philosophy*: "Dignytees," "regnes," "delyces of body," and "gentilesse." In this Boethian context, earthly love had been ranked with worthyness, royal estate, lust, and nobility as instances of the false world's brittleness. In the following stanzas he had replaced Boccaccio's practical advice on choosing a mistress with a Boethian *suasoria* to repair home from worldly vanity. Where Boccaccio had concluded this section of his poem by asking his audience to pray to Love for the repose of Troilus's soul—and for the grace to love prudently—Troilus had ended with a prayer to the Trinity.

Into this Boethian and Christian context Chaucer later inserted the *Teseida* stanzas describing Arcita's flight.Since they contained themes already explicit in his epilogue, he was able to adapt them to the *Troilus* with relatively minor changes: "The blynde lust, the which that may nat laste," and the words "blisfully" and "pleyn felicite." The first of these recalls the Boethian condemnation of the transitory pleasures of the world as well as the Christian conception of concupiscence as the desire for temporal and secular objects. The allusions to felicity reflect a commonplace of classical and Christian ethics. Stoic and Christian pneumatology had stressed the felicity of the separated soul. The knowledge of *vera felicitas* had been the ruling idea of Boethius's *Consolation*, and for Aristotle and his successors felicity not only constituted the true end or *fyn* of man but belonged in its highest form to the life of contemplation.

In this new context, the hero's ascent and freshly attained insight could serve as commentary on the entire poem. As a final appendix to the narrative, it could function as a concrete *exemplum*, providing inductive proof for the arguments already set forth in the final stanzas of the epilogue, emphasizing the *topoi* of worldly vanity and divine stability, *contemptus mundi* and love of God. As an extension of the formal catastrophe or "end" of the poem, it could underline the contrast between the true and false ends of man and the comparison of heavenly and earthly values. By inserting the flight episode at this point, Chaucer could stress not only the antithesis between the miserable end of the body and the happiness of the soul, but the additional contrast between mortal blindness and celestial knowledge, the opposition between the unstable felicity of the world and the changeless beatitude of heaven.

In thus heightening the contrast between permanent and transitory goods, these stanzas introduce a motif that is far more appropriate to the *Troilus* than to the Knight's Tale or even to the *Teseida*. In Boethius's *Consolation*, Dame Philosophy had based her indictment of *temporalia* and *terrena*—the goods of nature and the goods of fortune—primarily on the fact that they are subject to change. Worldly felicity is false because it is brittle and cannot endure. Throughout his romance, Chaucer has emphasized this point—by his own observations on Fortune, by Pandarus's counsel, by the reflections of the lovers themselves —and he has further heightened the motif of instability by stressing the contrast between the faithful and the unfaithful lover, juxtaposing Troilus's constancy to Criseyde's mutability. In the flight episode he presents the same antithesis in cosmic terms. Below the lunar sphere, in the elementary region, all is subject to alteration and mutability. Above the sphere of the moon, in the ethereal region, the heavens remain stable and constant, subject to neither generation nor corruption, immune to change. Having reached the lunar concave, Troilus stands on the threshold between mutability and immutability, and from this vantage point he can recognize the distinction between the abiding and the transitory, between the false felicity and the true. Here again Chaucer has altered Boccaccio's text—this time, to emphasize the theme of inconstancy. Boccaccio's references to the *tenebrosa cechitate* of mankind and the *falsa biltate* of the world have become the blind lust that "may not laste."

3

Happiness and misery are logical contraries, and by juxta-posing Troilus's miserable end with his vision of full felicity Chaucer not only emphasized the dichotomy of soul and body and the antithesis between earthly and heavenly goods but ac-centuated the distinction between the true and false ends of man. According to Boethian ethics, all men naturally desire felicity, but they are ignorant of its essential character and the way to achieve it. To awaken them to a recognition of their true nature and its end, to implant knowledge of the highest Good and of true happiness, is the divine mission of philosophy.

In his account of Troilus's illumination and in his exhortations to the "yonge . . . folkes" Chaucer retains the essential features of the Boethian system. Philosophy has chased "out of the sege of my corage alle covetise of mortel thynges";[2] Troilus similarly condemns the blind "lust" for temporal objects. Philosophy has reminded her pupil of "thilke commaundement of Pictagoras, that is to seyn, men schal serven to God, and noght to goddes";[3] Chaucer in turn condemns the service of the pagan deities and exhorts his readers to seek the true God. For Chaucer, as for Philosophy, "blisfulnesse" is "the soverayn good of nature that lyveth by resoun," and "the unstableness of fortune may nat atayne to resceyven verray blisfulnesse." Like Philosophy, he argues "how wrecchid is the blisfulnesse of mortel thynges, that neyther it dureth perpetuel with hem that every fortune resceyven agreablely or egaly, ne it deliteth nat in al to hem that ben angwyssous."[4] Like Philosophy, he demonstrates that the gifts of fortune (which are terminated by death) cannot offer true happiness and that full felicity is possible only after death: ". . . the soules of men ne mowen nat deyen in no wyse. . . . And syn we knowe wel that many a man hath sought the fruyt of blysfulnesse, nat oonly with suffrynge of death, but eek with

---

[2] Boethius, Book I, prose 4; F. N. Robinson, *The Works of Geoffrey Chaucer*, 2d ed. (Boston, 1957), p. 326.

[3] Boethius, Book I, prose 4.

[4] *Ibid.*, Book II, prose 4.

suffrynge of peynes and tormentz, how myghte thanne this present lif make men blisful, syn that whanne thilke selve lif es ended, it ne maketh folk no wrechches?"[5]

Both Chaucer and Boethius recognize the value of error for the discovery of truth, and the experience of false felicity as a stage toward knowledge of true happiness. Like Boethius's sight, Troilus's vision has been "ocupyed and destourbed by imagynacioun of erthly thynges" so that he cannot behold true felicity ("verray welefulnesse").[6] Like Boethius, after "byhooldyng ferst the false goodes," he withdraws his "nekke fro the yok of erthely affeccions" and achieves knowledge of "the verray goodes."[7] In the *Troilus* as in the *Consolation*, "the covetise of verray good is naturely iplauntyd in the hertes of men, but the myswandrynge errour mysledeth hem into false goodes."[8] All men "loken fro afar to thilke verray fyn of blisfulnesse." Though "naturel entencioun" leads them to the true good, they are misled by "many maner errours," seeking their natural end through money, honors, or other earthly goods.[9] Like Philosophy, Chaucer stresses the blindness of those who, ignorant of "where thilke goodes ben yhidd whiche that thei coveyten . . . ploungen hem in erthe, and seken there thilke good that surmounteth the hevene that bereth the sterris."[10] Like Philosophy, Chaucer portrays to his readers "the forme of fals welefulnesse" in order to "schewe the verray welefulnesse."[11] After getting the "false goodes with greet travaile," his hero comes to "knowen the verray goodes."[12]

The greater part of Dame Philosophy's catalogue of false goods recur in Chaucer's reflections on Troilus's *fyn*; by placing them in this context the poet emphasizes the fact that his hero had mistaken his true end.

[5] *Ibid.*, Book II, prose 4.
[6] *Ibid.*, Book III, prose 1.
[7] *Ibid.*, Book III, meter 1.
[8] *Ibid.*, Book III, prose 2.
[9] *Ibid.*, Book III, prose 3.
[10] *Ibid.*, Book III, meter 8.
[11] *Ibid.*, Book III, prose 9.
[12] *Ibid.*, Book III, meter 8.

Troilus's "grete worthynesse" had ended in death. The *Consolation* had devoted an entire section ("*set dignitatibus*") to this theme. "But dignytees," Philosophy inquires, "to whom thei ben comen, make they hym honourable and reverent?" Honors cannot render unworthy men "worthy of reverence," nor can true reverence come "by thise schadwy transitorie dignytes. . . ."[13]

Troilus's "estat real" had ended in death. "But regnes and familiarites of kynges," Philosophy continues, "mai thei maken a man to ben myghti? How elles, whan hir blisfulnesse dureth perpetuely? But certes the olde age of tyme passed, and ek of present tyme now, is ful of ensaumples how that kynges han chaungyd into wrecchidnesse out of hir welefulnesse. O, a noble thyng and a cleer thyng is power that is nat fownden myghty to kepe itself!"[14]

Troilus's "lust" terminates in death. "But what schal I seye of delyces of body, of whiche delices the desirynges ben ful of anguyssch, and the fulfillynges of hem ben ful of penance?" For Boethius's mentor, the "issues of delices ben sorweful and sorye. And yif thilke delices mowen maken folk blisful, thanne by the same cause moten thise beestis been clepid blisful, of which beestes al the entencioun hasteth to fulfille here bodily jolyte." Every delight "angwisscheth hem with prykkes that usen it." The man who leads his life in delights is despised as a "thral" to his body. "Now is it thanne wel yseyn how litil and how brotel possessioun thei coveyten that putten the goodes of the body aboven hir owene resoun." The beauty of the body, "how swyftly passynge is it, and how transitorie!" It is "more flyttinge than the mutabilite of floures of the somer sesoun"—an image that Chaucer would apply to the transitory world.[15]

---

[13] *Ibid.*, Book III, prose 4.

[14] *Ibid.*, Book III, prose 5.

[15] *Ibid.*, Book III, prose 7, meter 7, prose 8. In the first of these sections, Philosophy demonstrates, according to Pseudo-Aquinas, that beatitude does not consist in pleasure: "in qua philosophia ostendit beatitudinem non esse in voluptate." The desire for the pleasures of the body is a craving full of anxiety, since man feels anxiety when he lacks the object of his desire: "Quid

Troilus's "noblesse" likewise ends in death. "But now of this name of gentilesse, what man is it that ne may wele seen how veyn and how flyttinge a thyng it es? . . . For it semeth that

---

loquar de voluptatibus corporis id est delectationibus corporalibus: quarum appetentia id est cupiditas plena est anxietatis: quia homo anxiatur cum caret eo quod cupit." Even in the pleasure of matrimony there may be anxiety, and it cannot accordingly constitute true felicity: "Honestissima quidem coniugis foret. Hic philosophia ostendit quod beatitudo non consistit in quadam speciali voluptate .s. in matrimonio que licita est propter generationem prolis. intendens talem rationem. In illa voluptate non consistit felicitas que habet anxietatem sibi annexam. sed voluptas matrimonij est huiusmodi sicut tangit in littera." Next in meter 7 Philosophy shows that evil follows every pleasure: "in quo metro philosophia ostendit quid mali consequitur omnem voluptatem. omnis enim voluptas propter anxietatem sibi annexam est transitoria: quod confirmat per quoddam exemplum di[cens] Omnis voluptas habet quod dicam: quia voluptas agit .i. vexat fruentes stimulis .i. punitionibus [sic] & est par .i. similis stimulis apium volantum." "iocunditas voluptatis nimis est transitoria: sed anxietas quam affert nimis est permansura." "Notandum licet omnis voluptas corporalis primo delectet & postea pungat ad modum apium. cum hoc maxime invenitur in voluptate venerea ad cuius fugam Aristo[teles] hortatur Alexandrum di[cens] O clemens imperator noli te nimium inclinare ad coitum: quia coitus est quedam proprietas porcorum. que igitur tibi gloria si exerceas vicium bestiarum & actus brutorum." In prose 8 Philosophy demonstrates "quantis malis sunt implicita predicta bona in quibus aliqui posuerunt felicitatem. secundo ostendit quam exilia sunt corporis bona, . . voluptariam vitam degas: sed quis non spernat atque abijciat tanquam contemptibilem servum vilissimeque pro est fragilissime rei scilicet corporis. . . . Querens autem voluptuosam oportet quod corpori serviat . . . ."

Trivet's commentary gives essentially the same interpretation. In commenting on prose 7 he explains that "Primo ostendit propositum de voluptate generaliter. secundo de quadam speciali voluptate. que licitum est uti ordinate cuius est voluptas que consistit in actu matrimoniali. . . . Quod autem in voluptate non possit esse beatitudo probat dicens. Primo propter incommoda que comitantur voluptatem. secundo quia tunc beatitudo esseret in bestiis . . ." (fol. 145). "Primo igitur ostendens incommoda voluptatem concomitantia dicit. *Quid loquar de voluptatibus corporis* .s. iudicando [*or* indicando ?] eas inter ea que spectant ad beatitudinem quarum appetentia .i. cupiditas *plena est anxietatis*. anxiatur enim homo quum caret eo quod cupit" (fol 145). "Deinde cum dicit *honestissima* ostendit beatitudinem non esse illa beatitudine [*sic*] voluptate qua utuntur homines ordinate cuius est voluptas qua utitur homo secundum legem matrimonii . . . habet tamen anxietatem frequenter annexam. ratione cuius non potest in ea esse beatitudo" (fol. 145). In commenting on meter 7, Trivet asserts that in this meter philosophy shows "quid mali

gentilesse be a maner preisynge that cometh of the dessertes of auncestres; and yif preisynge make gentilesse, thenne mote they nedes ben gentil that been preysed. For which thing it folweth that yif thou ne have no gentilesse of thiself (*that is to seyn, prys that cometh of thy desert*), foreyn gentilesse ne maketh the nat gentil."[16]

Dignities, royal estate, gentilesse, delights of the body—these are transitory goods, and Boethius's celestial preceptress had condemned them specifically as false conceptions of beatitude. By deliberately inserting them between allusions to Troilus's "lovyng of Criseyde" and his miserable death, Chaucer has in a sense converted a story of unfortunate love into an *exemplum* of false felicity. The tale of one woman's inconstancy becomes a type of the inconstancy of the world; Criseyde's bad faith is emblematic of the faithlessness of Fortune. In the solicitude of the lover we find an instance of the Boethian *cura rerum temporalium*, and in his tragic end an example of the false world's brittleness. From his tragedy of secular love Chaucer has drawn the broadest possible *moralitas*: a condemnation that applies not only to the transitory pleasures of the flesh but to all "thise wrecched worldes appetites," and indeed to the world itself.

4

In the *Consolation of Philosophy*, Chaucer and Boccaccio encountered themes and images already well established in the

---

consequitur omnem voluptatem. Omnis enim voluptas propter anxietatem . . . est transitoria." "*Omnis voluptas habet hoc* .s. quod metro dicatur *agit* .i. vexat *fruentes stimulis* .i. anxiis punctionibus." "*Et ferit* .s. voluptas sic transiens *corda icta* .i. percussa anxietate *nimis tenaci morsu* q.d. iocunditas voluptatis est nimis transitoria. sed anxietas quam affert nimis permansura" (fol. 145). In commenting on prose 8, Trivet observes that "postquam philosophia ostendit quod vera beatitudo non consistit in istis bonis temporalibus in quibus homines posuerunt esse animi bonum: ostendit quot mala sint in adquisitione huiusmodi bonorum" (fol. 145). "*voluptariam vitam diligis* [*sic*]. *sed quis non spernat abjiciatque* .s. tamquam contemptibilem *servum vilissime fragilissimeque rei corporis* . . ." (fol. 146).

[16] *Ibid.*, Book III, prose 6.

apotheosis tradition. The flight of the mind to the heavens, the reorientation of thought and will from earthly to celestial objects, the contempt of the world and scorn of human folly, the blindness of humanity as to its true end and felicity—these motifs were characteristic of the *Consolation* as well as the flight episodes of Lucan and Dante and Cicero. The fact that these themes were common to both traditions made it easier to accommodate the conventions of the literary apotheosis to the Boethian context of the *Troilus* and the *Teseida*. Drawing on the imagery of both traditions, Chaucer and Boccaccio incorporated into their own flight sequences details reminiscent not only of the stellar voyages of Pompey and Scipio but also of the contemplative flights of Boethius's feathered philosophers. In the *Consolation* we may recognize images that we have already encountered in the literary apotheosis.

Like the *manes* of Pompey and Troilus and Arcita, Dame Philosophy and her initiates mount to the heights and, looking down from above, laugh at mankind's folly in pursuing the base and worthless values of the world ("At nos desuper inridemus vilissima rerum quaeque rapientes"): "But we that ben heghe above . . . we scorne swyche ravyneres and henteres of foulest thynges."[17] Pseudo-Aquinas interprets this passage in terms of the sage's contemplation of celestial objects and his laughter at worldly greed: "At nos sapientes in contemplatione celestium constituti irridemus malos rapientes. . . ."[18]

Philosophy's laughter is directed specifically to the cupidity and fury of evil men ("schrewes" and "wykkid folk"). Nevertheless, like other motifs in the *Consolation*, this convention (already well established in the philosophical literature of antiquity) could be applied to the pursuit of any false or earthly good: to the

---

[17] *Boethius*, trans. H. F. Stewart and E. K. Rand (London and New York, 1928), p. 140; Boethius, Book I, prose 3.

[18] Pseudo-Aquinas on Book I, prose 3, in *Boethius: Commentum duplex*; cf. Trivet, "*ac nos desuper* .i. in desiderio celestium constituti *irridemus* . . . sicut dicit psalmista qui habitat in celis irridebit eos *rapientes vilissima queque rerum terrena* . . ." (fol. 112).

craving for fame or riches or honors, to the desire for pleasure or worldly love, or (in its broadest application) to the entire complex of earthly values. The antithesis between *contemptus mundi* and *amor mundi*, which pervades Boethius's treatise and Chaucer's epilogue, receives concrete expression in the laughter of the classical sage or the mirth of the separated soul. The same contempt for the world and for "wrecched worldes appetites" recurs in Philosophy's derision of seekers after *vilissima rerum* and in Troilus's scorn of those who follow blind and transitory pleasures.

Like the *Somnium Scipionis* and the flight passages of Chaucer and Boccaccio, the *Consolation* stresses the magnitude of the heavens and the diminutive size of the earth in order to demonstrate the relative insignificance of worldly ends. The compass of the whole earth "ne halt but the resoun of a prykke at regard of the gretnesse of hevene"; and, by comparing the two, the mind may perceive "how litel and how voyde of alle prys is thylke glorye" of the world:[19]

Omnem terrae ambitum, sicuti astrologicis demonstrationibus accepisti, ad caeli spatium puncti constat obtinere rationem, id est ut, si ad caelestis globi magnitudinem conferatur, nihil spatii prorsus habere iudicetur.

Having demonstrated the vanity of worldly fame through an argument based on space, Philosophy now turns to an argument based on time. Since there can be no comparison between time and eternity, enduring fame on earth is actually of little moment: "But yow men semeth to geten yow a perdurablete, whan ye thynken that in tyme comynge your fame schal lasten. But natheles yif thow wolt maken comparysoun to the endles spaces of eternyte, what thyng hastow by which thow mayst rejoisen the of long lastynge of thi name?" Thousands of years "ne mai nat

---

[19] Stewart and Rand, p. 212; Boethius, Book II, prose 7. According to Pseudo-Aquinas (Book II, prose 7), "Hic philosophia ostendit gloriam mundanam esse exilem nec multum appetendam. primo ostendit hoc ex parte spacii in quo dilatatur. . . . No. terra respectu celi non est alicuius quantitatis sensibilis: sed habet se sicut punctus respectu circumferentie ipsius celi. . . ."

certes be comparysoned to the perdurablete that is endlees; for
. . . of thynges that ben withouten ende to thynges that han ende
may be makid no comparysoun."[20]

Finally, like Cicero's *Somnium Scipionis* and the flight sequences of Boccaccio and Chaucer, Boethius's treatise depicts
separated souls as indifferent to earthly cares. After demonstrating that earthly fame is vainglory, Philosophy argues that, if
the soul survives after death, it must regard "*renoun of this
world*"—and indeed all worldly values—as vain. Rejoicing in the
fruition of heaven, it scorns earthly affairs ("Sin vero bene sibi
mens conscia terreno carcere resoluta caelum libera petit, nonne
omne terrenum negotium spernat quae se caelo fruens terrenis
gaudet exemptam?"):[21]

And yif the soule, which that hath in itself science of gode werkes,
unbownden fro the prysone of the erthe, weendeth frely to the hevene,
despiseth it nat thanne al erthly ocupacioun; and, beynge in hevene,
rejoyseth that it is exempt fro alle erthly thynges?

In commenting on this passage, Pseudo-Aquinas paraphrases the
argument as follows: "Homines virtuosi vel totaliter moriuntur
corpore & anima: vel anima vivit post mortem[.] si totaliter
moriuntur nihil spectat ad eos de gloria post mortem. . . . Si
autem anima vivit post mortem: ista evolat ad celum & nihil curat
de fama: spernit omne terrenum negocium: & potius gaudet quia
est exempta a curis terrenis & gaudio celesti fruitur in eternum."[22]

If the man who regards glory as his "sovereyn good" (Philosophy continues) would only compare heaven and earth, looking
upon "the brode shewynge contrees of the hevene, and upon the
streyte sete of this erthe," he would be ashamed of "the encres of
his name, that mai nat fulfille the litel compas of the erthe."

---

[20] Boethius, Book II, prose 7.

[21] Stewart and Rand, pp. 216-218; Boethius, Book II, prose 7.

[22] Pseudo-Aquinas on Book II, prose 7, in *Boethius: Commentum duplex*;
cf. Trivet, "Quia virtuosi homines aut totaliter moriuntur. aut si vivit anima
post mortem petit celum. . . . Si vivunt [boni] cum sint in celo spernunt omne
terrenum. . . ." Cf. Stewart and Rand, pp. 216-218, "Sin vero bene sibi mens
conscia terreno carcere resoluta caelum libera petit, nonne omne terrenum
negotium spernat quae se caelo fruens terrenis gaudet exemptam?"

In these passages Dame Philosophy, like Scipio's guide in the *Somnium*, is inveighing primarily against the desire for earthly glory. Like Cicero, Boethius is exploiting the comparison between earth and heaven primarily in order to demonstrate the vanity of worldly fame. Nevertheless, the same argument could be directed against other temporal goods. In their treatment of the "earth-as-point" convention, as in their handling of the laughter motif, both Chaucer and Boccaccio made use of this *topos* to criticize the lover's mistaken judgment and his false estimation of genuine value. Boccaccio stressed the contrast between true and false beauty; Chaucer, the opposition between false goods and the sovereign Good. In both poems these motifs are closely associated, as in Boethius's treatise, with the soul's ascent to the heavens, its rejection of "omne terrenum negotium," and its fruition of celestial joy.

5

In asserting the vanity of earthly glory,[23] Philosophy had explicitly linked the wise man's contempt for the world with the felicity of souls after death. More frequently in the *Consolation*, however, she would apply such arguments to the preoccupations of the philosopher in this life. Exhorting the wise man to fix his mind on celestial ends and spurn temporal cares, she would portray the act of contemplation as a flight of the mind. Throughout the greater part of his treatise, Boethius treats the astral journey metaphorically, as an act of speculation, rather than literally, as an ascent of the spirit after death.

In his initial description of Dame Philosophy,[24] Boethius had stressed her celestial character: "sche touchede the hevene with the heghte of here heved; and whan sche hef hir heved heyer, sche percede the selve hevene so that the sighte of men lokynge was in ydel." In this metaphorical description ("pulsare caelum," "caelum penetrabat"),[25] Pseudo-Aquinas found an allusion to

[23] Boethius, Book II, prose 7.
[24] Boethius, Book I, prose 1.
[25] Stewart and Rand, p. 130.

Boethius's mathematical pursuits and his study of metaphysics—a science that directs its students to the knowledge of God and of separated substances ("inquantum dirigit in cognitionem dei & substantiarum separatarum".[26] Similarly, in describing Boethius's former study of astronomy, Dame Philosophy portrays him as metaphorically present in the heavens, observing the celestial bodies: "This man, that whilom was fre, to whom the hevene was opyn and knowen, and was wont to gon in hevenliche pathes, and saugh the lyghtnesse of the rede sonne, and saugh the sterres of the coolde mone, and which sterre in hevene useth wandrynge recourses iflyt by diverse speeris. . . ."[27]

In his commentary on this passage, Pseudo-Aquinas emphasized Boethius's former freedom from temporal cares and his ability to comprehend the planets by speculation: "liber .i. solutus a cura rerum temporalium celo sibi aperto per cognitionem suetus fuit ire per rationem ethereos meatus .i. in motus corporum celestium. . . . No. quod dic[it] celo aperto. licet homo planetas celi corporaliter non attingat: tamen speculatione comprehendit."[28]

Later in the treatise, Boethius adapted this motif to philosophical pursuits, principally the study of astronomy or of metaphysics. The flight motif may symbolize the study of the stars, but it may also represent the contemplation of the spiritual realm: the celestial intelligences, or God himself. If the opening portions of the *Consolation* emphasize the astronomical aspect of this metaphor, the latter portions of the work stress its metaphysical and theological reference. As Philosophy develops this image, it becomes a symbol of the intellectual love of God.

Describing the soul's reversion to its Creator "by ayenledynge fyer," Dame Philosophy implores divine assistance in leading the

---

[26] Pseudo-Aquinas on Book I, prose 1, in *Boethius: Commentum duplex*; cf. Trivet, "celum penetrabat tractando .s. de deo & angelis . . ." (fol. 108).

[27] Boethius, Book I, meter 2.

[28] Pseudo-Aquinas on Book I, meter 2, in *Boethius: Commentum duplex*; cf. Trivet, "*liber* i. solutus a cura temporalium *celo aperto* .s. per cognitionem quod clauditur per ignorantiam. *suetus* .i. assuetus *ire* .s. motu rationis disputando . . . *in ethereos meatus* .s. cursum corporis celestis . . ." (fol. 109).

mind back to its native heavens and the fruition of the Beatific Vision: "O thow Fadir, soowere and creatour of hevene and of erthes, that governest this world by perdurable resoun . . . thow that duellest thiselve ay stedefast and stable, and yevest alle othere thynges to ben meved. . . . O Fadir, yvye thou to the thought to steyen up into thi streyte seete; and graunte hym to enviroune the welle of good; and, the lyght ifounde, graunte hym to fycchen the clere syghtes of his corage in the; and skatere thou and tobreke the weyghtes and the cloudes of erthly hevynesse; . . . thow thiselfe art bygynnynge, berere, ledere, path and terme; to looke on the, that is our ende."[29] Arguing that "the sovereyne good is verray blisfulnesse" and that "verray blisfulnesse is set in sovereyn God,"[30] she exhorts mankind to return "*to this sovereyne good, that is God, that is refut to hem that wolen come to hym.*" To mortals bound "by the desceyvable delyt of erthly thynges" and "*combryd and desseyvid with worldly affeccions,*" this is "the reste of your labours," the "havene stable in pesible quiete," the "open refut to wreches."

For Philosophy, as for Chaucer, the vision of "the schynynge by which the hevene is governed" involves contempt for the world. The man who "may knowen thilke light of blisfulnesse, he schal wel seyn that the white beemes of the sonne ne ben nat cleer."[31] For the medieval poet, as for the classical moralist, true beatitude consists in the release of the soul from *fallax libido* and "blynde lust" and its return to the highest Good. In an earlier

[29] Boethius, Book III, meter 9.

[30] *Ibid.*, Book III, prose 10.

[31] *Ibid.*, Book III, meter 10. According to Pseudo-Aquinas, "in quo metro philosophia postquam ostendit in quo sit summa beatitudo: hortatur ad istam beatitudinem provenire dicens. Omnes capti quos fallax libido id est fallax delectatio habitans id est possidens terrenas mentes ligat improbis cathenis .i. viciosis cupiditatibus venite pariter huc .i. ad summum bonum quod est situm in deo." According to Trivet, in this meter philosophy exhorts men to seek true beatitude instead of the "falsa beatitudo" of temporal goods. "Dicit igitur o vos omnes capti . . . quos fallax libido .i. fallax delectacio habitans .i. frequentans mentes terrenas .i. terrenis deditas ligat improbis cathenis .i. viciosis cupiditatibus venite pariter . . . ad bonum & beatitudinem que ut ostensum est sita est in deo" (fol. 154).

passage Philosophy compares the transitory goods of the body with the magnitude and stability of the skies, governed by divine reason: "Byhoold the spaces and the stablenesse and the swyft cours of the hevene. . . ."[32] A similar contrast between the pleasures of the flesh and contemplation of the heavens underlies the posthumous experience of Arcita and Troilus. From the pursuit of earthly beauty they turn to the contemplation of the stars. Deprived of carnal enjoyment, they become amateur astronomers.

Subsequently, Boethius's instructress describes the ascent of the mind, promising to "fycchen fetheris in thi thought, by which it mai arisen in heighte" and "retourn hool and sownd into thi contree."[33] When "the swifte thoght" has clothed itself in Philosophy's feathers, "it despiseth the hateful erthes, and surmounteth the rowndnesse of the gret ayr; and it seth the clowdes byhynde

---

[32] Boethius, Book III, prose 8. In Philosophy's demonstration of the baseness and vileness of the goods of the body (Book III, prose 8), Pseudo-Aquinas finds a double argument from magnitude and from beauty. The first of these involves a comparison with the heavens: "Hic philosophia probat in speciali quod vilia sunt bona corporis que aliqui reputant egregia bona. . . . Primo ostendit intentum de magnitudine: fortitudine: & corporis agilitate. Secundo de pulchritudine. . . . Primo ostendit quod homo non debet mirari de magnitudine fortitudine: et agilitate corporis quia illa excellentius inveniuntur in brutis quam in hominibus: \ . . . Respice spacium id est magnitudinem celi: firmitudine [sic] id est fortitudinem celi: celeritatem .i. velocitatem eius. et aliquando desinite .i. cessate mirari vilia .i. inferiora bona. . . ." "Forme vero nitor. Hic philosophia ostendit intentum de pulchritudine forme scilicet quod sit exile bonum quia est transitoria & quia tantum est superficialis & dicit. vero pro sed nitor id est pulchritudo forme ut id est quam rapidus est: ut id est quam velox .i. velociter est transiens: & est fugacior id est mutabilior mutabilitate florum vernalium." Cf. Trivet, "*Iam vero* hic speciali[ter] ostendit quam exilia sunt corporis bona (fol. 146). Considering the relative magnitude, strength, agility, and beauty of the goods of the body, Philosophy demonstrates that men ought not to admire them ("admirari") as truly excellent: "cum dicit *respice* docet quanta non sunt miranda in comparacione ad rationem" (fol. 146). Cf. Stewart and Rand, pp. 252-254, "Respicite caeli spatium, firmitudinem, celeritatem et aliquando desinite vilia mirari. Quod quidem caelum non his potius est quam sua qua regitur ratione mirandum."

[33] Boethius, Book IV, prose 1.

his back, and passeth the heighte of the regioun of the fir. . . ."
Having returned to the heaven of the "lord of kynges," the soul at
last recognizes its true country ("of which thou ne haddest no
mynde") and resolves that *"here wol I duelle."* From this altitude
it may look back "on the derknesse of the erthe" that it had left
behind and perceive that tyrants "schullen ben exiled fro thilke
faire contre."[34]

At another stage of the argument Dame Philosophy contrasts
the philosopher's vision with the blindness of ordinary men, who
mistake their true felicity. The latter "have hir eien so wont to the
derknesse of erthly thinges that they ne may nat lyften hem up to
the light of cler sothfastnesse." Such men, "loke nat the ordre of
thinges, but hir lustes and talentz [appetites]. . . ." To the
philosopher, however, who contemplates both "the fowle erthe
and the hevene," it seems "as by oonly resoun of lokynge, that
thow were now in the sterres and now in the erthe. But the peple
ne loketh nat on these thinges."[35]

Finally, exhorting her followers ("ye stronge men") to *"wyn-
nen the mede of the hevens,"* Philosophy promises that "the erthe
overcomen yeveth the sterres. (*This to seyn, that whan that erthly
lust is overcomyn, a man is makid worthy to the hevene.*)"[36]

The principal motifs of Chaucer's flight passage—Troilus's
ascent to the heavens, his observation of the "erratik sterres," his
downward glance to "This litel spot of erthe," his contempt for
"This wrecched world," his laughter at the folly of mankind and
at temporal cares, his final insight into "pleyn felicite"—these had
all been anticipated by Dame Philosophy in her *consolatio.*
Belonging alike to Boethian convention and to the literary apotheosis, they link Chaucer's epilogue firmly with both traditions.

Also characteristic of Boethian tradition are the themes of the

---

[34] *Ibid.*, Book IV, meter 1.
[35] *Ibid.*, Book IV, prose 4.
[36] *Ibid.*, Book IV, meter 7. In man's upright stature, Philosophy finds an
additional argument for despising earthly objects and seeking a heavenly good.
Unlike the beasts of the earth, man alone "heveth heyest his heie heved, and
stondith light with his upryght body, and byholdeth the erthes undir hym"
(Book V, meter 5).

original epilogue. In addition to the instances of the world's "brotelnesse" in the *fyn* stanza, Chaucer's awareness of "so gret diversite" in his spoken and written "tonge" (and perhaps of the analogy with "the forme of olde clerkes speche In poetrie") is likewise reminiscent of a Boethian commonplace. In the *Consolation*, Dame Philosophy includes diversity of speech and the fate of ancient writings among her arguments against desire for earthly glory:

And also set this therto: that many a nacioun, diverse of tonge and of maneris. . . ben enhabited in the cloos of thilke lytel habitacle: to the which nacyons, what for . . . diversity of langages . . . nat oonly the names of synguler men ne may nat strecchen, but eek the fame of citees ne may nat strecchen.

Moreover, "thilke wrytynges profiten litel, the whiche writynges long and dirk eelde doth awey, bothe hem and ek hir auctours!"[37]

   In the final stanzas of the epilogue the poet combines Boethian and Christian doctrines. If his prayer to "that sothfast Crist, that starf on rode," springs from his Catholic faith, his emphasis on God's fidelity:

> For he nyl falsen no wight, dar I seye,
> That wol his herte al holly on hym leye

reflects Boethius's insistence on the Creator's "stable feyth" as well as Christian orthodoxy. Near the close of the *Consolatio*, Dame Philosophy delivers a final exhortation to her disciple:[38] "Ne in ydel ne in veyn ne ben ther put in God hope and preyeris, that ne mowen nat ben unspedful ne withouten effect whan they been ryghtful." To an early Renaissance commentator this passage held the key to the intent of the entire work. In Ascensius's opinion, the *Consolation* attempted, *inter alia*, to inculcate a disregard for mortal things and to justify divine providence, dispelling the erroneous opinion that God does not govern justly:[39]

dum quia iniuste patimur: deum aut non curare mortalia: aut non recte gubernare falsò opiniamur: in hoc eum [enim?] totum opus conclu-

---

[37] *Ibid.*, Book II, prose 7.
[38] *Ibid.*, Book V, prose 6.
[39] Ascensius, "Proemium," in *Boethius: Commentum duplex*.

ditur cum dicitur. Nec frustra sunt in deo posite spes precesque que cum recte fiunt inefficaces esse non possunt.

Like Boethius, Chaucer ends his work with an affirmation of divine fidelity, in contrast with the faithlessness of the world.

Even the final prayer to the Trinity—a passage derived from Dante—does not altogether violate the Boethian framework of the *Troilus*. In the *Consolation*, Dame Philosophy herself addresses more than one devout prayer to the Creator and Governor of the universe—the beginning, the way, and the end of all things—and to many of Chaucer's contemporaries Boethius himself was the author of a treatise on the Trinity. Dante regarded him as a martyr and a saint.

In Philosophy's discourses, as in the final stanzas of Chaucer's epilogue, exhortations to true felicity tend to predominate over dissuasions from false happiness. In identifying the supreme Good as God himself and in regarding the *visio dei* as the true end and felicity of man, Boethius's instructress comes very close to scholastic conceptions of beatitude. When compared with her exhortations, especially those of Book Three, the Christian elements in Chaucer's epilogue appear to be thoroughly consistent with the Boethian values of his poem.

Although Troilus eventually achieves a philosopher's insight into true and false felicity, there is one significant difference between his celestial ascent and that of the Boethian sage. Like other heroes of the apotheosis tradition, Troilus makes his journey to the heavens after death. During his own lifetime he has been notably ignorant of his true felicity and end. Unlike the Stoic or Neoplatonic wise man, or the Boethian *sapiens* liberated by the study of philosophy, Troilus has been unaware of his true "hom," and "contre"—that celestial *patria* to which Dame Philosophy exhorts her disciple and Chaucer his audience of "yonge . . . folkes." Only after death does he return to the regions that the Boethian sage may visit, in his own lifetime, through intellectual contemplation. Troilus learns by experience what Boethius has learned through the tutelage of Dame Philosophy and what Chaucer's readers might presumably learn vicariously from Chaucer's epilogue and from the *exemplum* of Troilus himself.

In contrast to the metaphorical journey that Dame Philosophy urges her followers to undertake, the speculative flight of the mind, Troilus's journey is the posthumous flight of a separated soul. Unlike Boethius and Dante, he has chosen Criseyde, rather than Dame Philosophy or Beatrice, as his sovereign lady or *domina*; and in pursuing his earthly beatitude he has had only Pandarus to guide him. With the wretched end of body and bodily affection, worldly romance and worldly dignities, he finally learns the true end of the rational soul. This consists, significantly, neither in earthly pleasure nor in worldly action, but in celestial contemplation.

6

In juxtaposing Troilus's miserable death with his insight into true felicity, Chaucer gave concrete expression to the tension between naïve and philosophical, worldly and otherworldly, conceptions of the end or *fyn* of man. The lover's end or felicity —the physical possession of his mistress—has proved to be false and transitory. Noble birth and royal estate are likewise transitory; they belong to the world and terminate with death. Chaucer brings all of these false ends into the context of the hero's "pitous" death, the traditional "wretched ending" of tragedy, contrasting them with the celestial beatitude that, according to classical philosophy and Christian theology, constitutes the true end of man.

By thus centering the epilogue on the contrast between true and false conceptions of happiness, the poet has been faithful not only to Boethian values but also to the theoretical ends of his art, to the traditional relationship between poetry and moral philosophy. For Dante, the "end" or final cause of the *Commedia* had been human beatitude: to "remove those living in this life from the state of misery and lead them to the state of felicity." His poem had been regulated, he declared, by a branch of philosophy, "morals or ethics." Perhaps Chaucer, who dedicated the *Troilus* to "moral" Gower and "philosophical" Strode and who exploited the antithesis between misery and beatitude in the epilogue to his own poem, regarded the *Troilus* in a similar light.

Unlike Dante and Boethius, Chaucer did not personify philosophy or theology; there are no Dame Philosophy and no Beatrice in his romance. Nevertheless Troilus's final insights come close to those of the Boethian philosopher and the scholastic theologian. The contrast between the states of misery and felicity is no less central to the epilogue of the *Troilus* than to the *Commedia*. For Pseudo-Aquinas, indeed, this contrast was also fundamental for for the *Consolation*. The subject matter of this treatise, in his opinion, was Boethius's wretched condition and Philosophy's consolation: "status miserabilis Boe. philosophica consolatione superinducta."[40]

Common to all three works, moreover, was an emphasis on true felicity and security and on contempt of worldly values. Summarizing Seneca's exhortations to the study of philosophy[41] —"ut tibi contingat vera libertas: ut tibi contingat vera securitas: ut tibi notescat felicitas: ut par deo fias"—Pseudo-Aquinas attempted to demonstrate the truth of these propositions by syllogistic reasoning. Philosophy bestows knowledge of beatitude, the final end of man: "Nam ultimus finis vite humane est beatitudo: cuius cognitionem philosophia tradit." The consolation of philosophy (which is the material cause of Boethius's treatise) attempts to arouse contempt for worldly things and to awaken desire for the highest felicity: "philosophica consolatio ordinata ad contemptum mundanorum & ad appetitum summe felicitatis."[42] The same words could be applied, with almost equal justice, to Dante's comedy and to the epilogue of Chaucer's tragedy.

For Pseudo-Aquinas, as for Aristotle, philosophy is the knowledge of truth ("scientiam veritatis"), leading man from the darkness of ignorance to the light of wisdom: "Et philosophia trahit hominem ab obscuritate ignorantie ad scientiam: a tenebris stulticie ad lucem sapientie & ad claritatem intellectus."[43] The progression from ignorance to knowledge is also common to all

---

[40] Pseudo-Aquinas, "Proemium," in *ibid*.
[41] Pseudo-Aquinas, *ibid*.
[42] Pseudo-Aquinas, *ibid*.
[43] Pseudo-Aquinas, *ibid*.

three works, though the imagery of light and darkness is less marked in Chaucer's poem than in the *Commedia* and the *Consolation*, or, indeed, the flight passages of Lucan and Boccaccio.

Finally, Pseudo-Aquinas distinguishes sharply between two different kinds of felicity: political and speculative. The first consists in external goods and is by nature unstable. The second, conversely, is stable and immutable and consists in an act of wisdom: the contemplation of substances separated from matter (such as the realm of ideal essences or pure spirits):[44] "Alia est felicitas speculativa que consistit in actu sapientie: scilicet in speculatione substantiarum separatarum: et talis felicitas est stabilis & immutabilis: cum sit bonum optimum pulcerrimum: delectabilissimum. ex primo ethicorum." This distinction is of basic importance for the theme and structure of the *Commedia*. Whether or not Pseudo-Aquinas was justified in reading it into the *Consolation* is a different matter, however, and we should be cautious in applying this distinction to the epilogue of Chaucer's poem. It does, nevertheless, underline the essential difference between the unstable and transitory felicity Troilus has enjoyed on earth—the external goods whose mutability is emphasized by the reiterated stress on *fyn*—and the *felicitas speculativa* he enjoys in heaven.

With this distinction in mind, let us turn to Aristotle's discussion of felicity. Though the Boethian frame of reference is most apparent in the *Troilus*, Aristotelian influences had reshaped scholastic theology, and, directly or indirectly, Chaucer could hardly have escaped some contact with the principal doctrines of the *Nicomachean Ethics*. Pseudo-Aquinas, moreover, had interpreted the *Consolation* against a broad and varied background, in the light of Aristotle as well as Seneca and Cicero and other moralists.

Distinguishing three principal types of life—voluptuous, active (or political), and contemplative—according to their respective

---

[44] Pseudo-Aquinas on Book I, meter 1, in *ibid*.

ends, Aristotle had given the highest rank to the third. Identifying happiness with pleasure, the *vita voluptaria* was (he maintained) "a life suitable to beasts. . . ." Equating happiness with honor or virtue, the *vita activa*, in turn, exercised the practical virtues "in political or military affairs"; nevertheless, it could not bestow perfect felicity.[45] Of all three lives, the *vita contemplativa* offered the highest felicity, inasmuch as "perfect happiness is a contemplative activity" and since "the activity of God, which surpasses all others in blessedness, must be contemplative." Because "happiness extends . . . just as far as contemplation does, and those to whom contemplation more fully belongs are more truly happy," the philosopher must necessarily be "the happiest" of men and "the dearest to the gods."[46]

In his meditation on Troilus's end, Chaucer dismisses as worldly vanities certain values of the voluptuous and active lives, but not those of the contemplative life. Troilus's "love" and "lust" belong to the life of pleasure; his royal condition, his worthiness, and his nobility pertain to the active or political life. Throughout the poem, Chaucer has devoted his primary attention to the *vita voluptaria*, describing the hero's "love" rather than his "armes." Troilus's exploits in the *vita activa* receive cursory treatment; they are primarily significant for the narrative in their relationship to his love affair. His struggle with philosophical paradoxes beyond the capacity of his years ends in failure; he exercises the contemplative virtues, like the active virtues, primarily in relation to his passion for Criseyde. In the flight stanzas, however, he finally achieves the characteristic privileges of a philosopher, contemplating the heavens and attaining a philosopher's insight into the

[45] Richard McKeon, ed., *The Basic Works of Aristotle* (New York, 1941), pp. 938, 1105; *Ethica Nicomachea*, trans. W. D. Ross.

[46] McKeon, *Aristotle*, pp. 1106-1108. According to the *Metaphysics* (trans. Ross; McKeon, *Aristotle*, p. 693), the "most honorable" of all sciences must be "the most divine science"—the science that is "most meet for God to have" and that "deals with divine objects. . . . " Aristotle's claims on behalf of metaphysics as the "most divine" science would subsequently be reiterated by Christian schoolmen on behalf of theology.

distinction between true and false goods. The "pleyn felicite" he encounters in the heavens is the traditional happiness of the *vita contemplativa*.[47]

Thus far we have reexamined Chaucer's flight sequence in its relationship to two related, but diverse traditions: the apotheosis of the hero after death and the speculative flight of the moral or metaphysical philosopher in this life. Troilus's flight incorporates motifs common to both traditions, and the "pleyn felicite" he encounters in the heavens is not only "the state of [virtuous] souls after death"—to echo Dante—but the speculative happiness that Philosophy had promised her followers as their final end, in this life as well as the next. In contemplating the heavens, Troilus encounters the characteristic felicity enjoyed by students of the "divine science" during their own lifetime, as well as the beatitude of separated souls.

From the relationship of the flight stanzas to the Boethian values of the poem as a whole and to the themes and structure of the original epilogue, let us turn finally to problems of literary technique.

---

[47] In Saint Augustine's opinion, the *summum bonum* was the end of ethics and indeed of "all philosophy." For Plato (Augustine continues) the highest good is God, "and therefore he will have a philosopher a lover of God, that, because philosophy aims at beatitude, the lover of God might be blessed by enjoying God." See John M. Steadman, *Milton's Epic Characters*, (Chapel Hill, N.C., 1968), pp. 106-107.

CHAPTER VII

THE CONCLUSION OF THE *TROILUS* NARRATIVE AND COMMENTARY

To many readers Chaucer's epilogue has seemed both prolix and confused. The poet as commentator (it would appear) is engaged in a running debate with himself as narrator. Each is endeavoring to outargue the other, each is striving to speak the last word. Chaucer seems to be chasing his own tale. In the last fifteen stanzas of the poem, incident and *envoi* are intermixed. In the strictest sense, the story does not end until the poet has apologized to the ladies for portraying an unfaithful woman, added a few cautionary lines warning them against betrayers, and formally bidden farewell to his book. At this point he returns to his narrative, relating Troilus's wrath,[1] death, and apotheosis. After a brief sententious commentary on the hero's end, he terminates the story with a recapitulation of the argument:

> And thus bigan his lovyng of Criseyde,
> As I have told, and in this wise he deyde.

Here, like a reluctantly departing guest who, hat in hand, has detained us on the doorstep with a final anecdote, Chaucer drops the narrative and turns once more to the urgent problem of leave-taking. Drawing the moral inferences his contemporaries might have expected, and would certainly have approved, he concludes his romance with direct appeals to his varied audience. This is an unusually long epilogue, even for a rather long story, and to some of Chaucer's critics the coda wags the poem.

Disproportionate in length, the epilogue may also seem inconsistent with the earlier portions of the romance in structure,

---

[1] In describing Troilus's "wraththe" after his betrayal by Criseyde, Chaucer shifts his emphasis from the concupisible to the irascible appetite or faculty. According to Robert Burton, *The Anatomy of Melancholy* (London, 1837), I:156, "All affections and perturbations arise out of these two fountains. . . ."

mood, and theme. Structurally, it introduces an ending that apparently converts the human tragedy into a divine comedy. The mood likewise veers from tragic to comic sensibility; the poet shifts from one form of pathetic proof to its opposite, from vicarious involvement in the joys and sorrows of the lovers to an attitude of cosmic indifference and Olympian ridicule. Thematically (it would appear) the epilogue is a retractation, a rejection of the basic values of the narrative and a renunciation of "courtly love." Its Christian elements seem inconsistent with the pagan setting of the story. Its denunciation of "thise wrecched worldes appetites" seems out of place in a love story—as incongruous as mirth at a funeral or mourning at a wedding feast. Subjecting the conventions of chivalric romance to the dry light of classical metaphysics and scholastic theology, the epilogue dismisses the felicity and misery of the lovers as equally vain and meaningless. Under the harsh insights of philosophy, Chaucer's muses, like those of Boethius, stand abashed and discountenanced; they can only take refuge in flight.

1

If Homer can nod occasionally, so perhaps can Chaucer. In the epilogue, however, he shows every sign of being thoroughly wide awake. The contradictions that Curry[2] deplored seem to be negligible, if not imaginary. In many instances they result either

---

[2] Cf. Walter Clyde Curry, *Chaucer and the Mediaeval Sciences* (New York, 1960), pp. 294-298: "What follows in the Epilog to the completed drama . . . is dramatically a sorry performance. . . . Here in the Epilog the poet, without having given the slightest hint of warning, suddenly denies and contradicts everything that has gone before in the poem. The love-affair of Troilus and Criseyde, which he has presented with gusto and which we have watched with sympathy develop into a tragedy, is now condemned as worldly vanity. . . . But Chaucer is not yet content with that nest of contradictions, the Epilog; having finished his sermon, he must needs return to his manuscript and insert the three stanzas (V, 1807-27) which represent the flight of Troilus's spirit through the heavens to the realm of true felicity. . . . One may deplore, therefore, the tendency of certain critics to interpret the action of the whole story in the light of this entirely contradictory Epilog, with the result that the tragic quality of the poem is blurred and the supreme artistry of it vitiated."

from intentional irony—a quality that Chaucer shares with Lu-can[3] and Boethius—or from a deliberate mixture of sententious and narrative materials. Elsewhere in his poetry he employs similar techniques, mixing profit with delight, breaking the momentum of the narrative to increase suspense, and relying on his readers' interest in the story to carry them through the didactic passages. By thus interweaving narrative episode and moral observation, he accentuates the thematic relationships between narrative *exemplum* and ethical generalization. The events themselves provide the moral *topoi* for his commentary.

The interweaving of narrative and sententious material is notably absent in the final stanzas of the *Filostrato*; and the greater complexity of Chaucer's ending results largely from his conscious transformation of his source. Though he partly retained the outline of Boccaccio's conclusion—the summary of Troilo's final gests and death, the reflections on his tragic *fine*, and the address to the *giovanetti*—Chaucer made numerous interpolations within this framework besides adding the concluding invocations. By inserting his apology and *envoi* before the account of Troilus's death, he broke the continuity of the narrative; and by interpolating the flight passage he separated Boccaccio's report of Troilo's death from the moral observations on his end. The apparent looseness of Chaucer's epilogue springs directly from his innovations on the *Filostrato*.

Chaucer could not, in fact, retain the structure of Boccaccio's ending without also retaining its thematic content. Having decided to end his poem in a less frivolous vein than that of his principal source, he was compelled to transform the structure of Boccaccio's epilogue. Even before inserting the flight stanzas, he

---

[3] Cf. D. W. Robertson, Jr., *A Preface to Chaucer: Studies in Medieval Perspectives* (Princeton, 1963), p. 288; Charles Berryman, "The Ironic Design of Fortune in *Troilus and Criseyde*," *Chaucer Review*, II (1967), 1-7; Anthony E. Farnham, "Chaucerian Irony and the Ending of the *Troilus*," *Chaucer Review*, I (1967), 207-216; Ida L. Gordon, "The Narrative Function of Irony in Chaucer's *Troilus and Criseyde*," *Medieval Miscellany Presented to Eugène Vinaver*, ed. R. Whitehead, A. H. Diverres, and F. E. Sutcliffe (Manchester and New York, 1965), pp. 146-156.

had radically altered Boccaccio's reflections on Troilo's *mal concetto amore* and the cynical advice to the young men. He had discarded many of Boccaccio's *topoi*, substituting arguments drawn from moral philosophy and theology. Having increased the "specific gravity" of the epilogue, he could not retain Boccaccio's framework without sacrificing balance and proportion. He could preserve its structure only in a very limited degree.

In structuring his own epilogue, Chaucer appropriately followed the order of climax, placing his lighter and less serious passages near the beginning and deferring the graver topics for the end. Accordingly, he inserted the half humorous addresses to the gentlewomen and to his book *before* the account of Troilus's death. Even though this arrangement resulted in interrupting the narrative and in separating these passages from later appeals to his audience, it would seem to be justified by the very different tone of these early addresses and the later appeals to the "yonge . . . folkes," to Gower and Strode, and to the Trinity. Chaucer could hardly have placed either the *envoi* to his book or the apology to the ladies at a later point in the epilogue. To have grouped them with the final addresses to his audience—to have placed them *after* Troilus's death and apotheosis—would have weakened the force of his final exhortations, undermining the gravity and moral intensity of his concluding stanzas.

2

The techniques whereby Chaucer interlarded narrative and sententious material, interrupting his story for moral comment or direct appeals to his audience, reflect the principles of rhetorical amplification or abbreviation. (They should not, of course, be confused with the *entrelacement* whereby medieval and Renaissance poets attempted to interweave or "interlace" the various strands of their narrative into a closely, or loosely, knit whole.) Though classical rhetoricians frequently interpreted these terms in a *qualitative* sense (applying them, for instance, to techniques for aggravating or extenuating the importance of an action), medieval rhetoric and poetic tended to emphasize their *quantitative* sense, applying them specifically to the expansion or contraction of the writer's material.[4] In amplifying his subject matter, the poet might resort to apostrophe, description, or comparison; to similes and other forms of digression; to figures of repetition, and similar rhetorical devices. In contracting or abridging his material, however, he would deliberately avoid such techniques.

The mixture of narrative and authorial commentary was likewise conventional both in theory and in practice. By temporarily interrupting his story to express his own opinion, the poet could introduce ethical or pathetic proof. By inserting moral commonplaces or *sententiae* into the narrative, or into the speeches of his characters, he might heighten the didactic content of a passage or increase its persuasive force. Such "sentences" might function as enthymemes, or incomplete syllogisms, and could therefore serve as logical proof. Finally, the poet might directly exhort or "dehort" his readers, introducing *suasoriae* or *dissuasoriae* at the end of the poem or within the narrative itself. In the same way, he might interpolate passages of accusation or apology, and praise or blame.

Some of the principal similarities and differences in the endings of the *Filostrato* and the *Troilus* have already been noted. They will now be reexamined in terms of the techniques of *amplificatio* (*dilatatio* or *augmentatio*) and *abbreviatio* (*deminutio* or *attenuatio*).

After Pandaro's final speech, Boccaccio drastically contracts his narrative. Briefly summarizing Troilo's grief and anger, the poet reduces the slaughter of myriads of Greeks to a few verses and the hero's death to a single line. He does not describe any of the numerous battles in which his protagonist proved his knighthood. He does not delineate the battlefield where Troilo met his fate or relate the circumstances of his death. He does not record the hero's last words or final thoughts. He reserves the techniques of amplification until the end of the narrative, exploiting a figure of repetition (anaphora) to emphasize the misery of Troilo's *fine*,

---

[4] Cf. Edmond Faral, ed., *Les arts poétiques du XIIe et du XIIIe siècle* (Paris, 1958), pp. 61-85.

dilating on the theme of woman's inconstancy in his appeal to the *giovanetti*, and devoting the last section of his poem to his *envoi* to his book.

With two exceptions—the three flight stanzas and the expansion of a single stanza in his source into two (250-251)— Chaucer retains Boccaccio's highly abbreviated version of the story. For the most part, his amplifications consist in addresses (not all of them are true apostrophes) to various persons or objects: the gentlewomen, his book, the "yonge . . . folkes," Gower and Strode, and "the Lord." The apparent inconsistency, or incoherence, of the epilogue results from the fact that Chaucer has not only greatly increased the number of such appeals (giving us *five* such addresses, all to different recipients, where the *Filostrato* was content with two), but that, unlike Boccaccio, he has broken the continuity of his narrative by inserting two of these passages before finishing the actual story. For a modern reader this may be confusing; for an audience accustomed to a mixture of narrative and sententious elements and to the frequent interruption of the narrative through the devices of amplification, it would be understandable and perhaps not unexpected.

To the more judicious reader, familiar with techniques of augmentation and contraction, the awareness of how much Chaucer has contracted that he could have amplified, and vice versa, would be an additional guide to the values that the poet considered most important, Summarizing Troilus's death in a single line, Chaucer devotes three stanzas to his ascent to the heavens and his insight into true felicity, and the six remaining stanzas to the antithesis between worldly vanity and the steadfastness of the Christian God. To a careful reader, the quantitative proportions of the epilogue would indicate the themes the poet wished to emphasize.

In the earlier version of the epilogue, the relationship between the narrative passages and the passages of authorial comment would hardly have seemed confusing. Though the interpolation of the apology to the ladies and the poet's farewell to his book may complicate the structure, their relationship to the story remains sufficiently clear; it should not have perplexed an audience used to much longer digressions. The three final addresses, in turn, occur after the death of the protagonist and hence do not interrupt the narrative at all. Their position in the formal structure of the epilogue should have been unambiguous. Nor do the flight stanzas interrupt the narrative. They merely extend the story of Troilus a little farther, from this life into the next. After reporting the death of the hero's body, the poet concludes by narrating the fate of his soul. Though this passage breaks the original continuity between the account of Troilus's death and the reflections on his end, the insertion itself provides an additional link between them. The *fyn* stanza follows, reasonably enough, immediately after Troilus's survey of the scene of his death, his laughter at the grief of his mourners, and his condemnation of worldly vanities. Although Chaucer's interpolation has misled one twentieth-century critic, it effectively links the story of Troilus's death with the argument of the *fyn* stanza and the poet's final addresses *in propria persona*.

The values Chaucer wished to emphasize in the conclusion of his poem are evident in the material he chose to amplify or contract. Both in his principal narrative addition (the flight stanzas themselves) and in his passages of commentary or direct address, his major emphasis falls on the antithesis between earthly felicity and celestial beatitude. The "diffuseness" of his epilogue is a modern accusation; medieval or Renaissance critics would have called it "copiousness."

3

Among the problems the critic must face in considering the thematic or structural coherence of Chaucer's epilogue[5] are the

---

[5] In addition to studies already cited, see S. Nagarajan, "The Conclusion to Chaucer's *Troilus and Criseyde*," *Essays in Criticism*, XIII (1955), 174-177; E. Talbot Donaldson, "The Ending of Chaucer's *Troilus*," in *Early English and Norse Studies Presented to Hugh Smith in Honour of his Sixtieth Birthday*, ed. Arthur Brown and Peter Foote (London, 1963), pp. 26-45; Karl Young, "Chaucer's Renunciation of Love in *Troilus*," *MLN*, XL (1925), 270-276; Alan T. Gaylord, "Chaucer's Tender Trap: The *Troilus* and the 'Yonge,

questions of extent[6] and intent—the uncertainty as to where, precisely, the epilogue begins, and whether the term itself may not, in fact, be misleading.

Since the narrative does not end until the account of Troilus' death (Stanza 258) and apotheosis (259-261) and the author's final summary of his argument at the end of the *fyn* stanza (262), one might plausibly restrict the "epilogue" to the last five stanzas, in which the author addresses the "yonge . . . folkes," Gower and Strode, and the Trinity. Nevertheless, the fact that Chaucer has placed his apology and his *envoi* immediately before these narrative passages would appear to argue against this comparatively modest conception of the epilogue.

Where then does the epilogue actually begin? One could locate its beginning with the *envoi* (stanzas 256-257), but this passage is preceded by the author's apology; and in the following stanza (258) he returns to the theme of Troilus' "wraththe," a topic he had raised in stanza 251 and temporarily dropped after stanza 253. The apology might constitute a suitable beginning, but it likewise interrupts the narrative account of Troilus's wrath. Moreover, it belongs grammatically with the preceding stanza. Virtually the entire first stanza of this passage is a participial phrase, modifying a personal pronoun in stanza 253. Nor do the stanzas immediately following Pandarus's discomfiture consti-

---

Fresshe Folkes,'" *English Miscellany*, XV (1964), 27; Elizabeth K. Reedy, "'This Litel Spot of Erthe': Time and 'Trouthe' in Chaucer's *Troilus and Criseyde*," DA 28 (1967).

[6] John S. P. Tatlock, "The Epilog of Chaucer's *Troilus*," MP, XVIII (1920-1921), 113-114, regards the last *twelve* stanzas (stanzas 256-267) as "a diffused Epilog or *envoi*, mingled with the completion of the story" and composed of six parts: (1) the poet's adieu to his book; (2) his prayer that its text and verse may escape corruption; (3) Troilus's death and ascent; (4) the exhortation to the young; (5) the address to Gower and Strode; and (6) the "devotional invocation to the Trinity. . . ." Tatlock's essay is concerned primarily with the first, fourth, and fifth parts. In Stroud's opinion (pp. 1-9) the epilogue consists of "two opposed but self-contained conclusions, separated by the narrative (Troilus' death and ascent)." Curry (p. 294) restricts the epilogue to lines 1807-1869—that is, to the last *nine* stanzas (stanzas 259-267). Sanford B. Meech, *Design in Chaucer's Troilus* (Syracuse, 1959), pp. 129-138, divides "the ending into two segments," lines 1541-1771 and lines 1772-1869.

tute an altogether satisfactory beginning. Stanza 250 summarizes Troilus's position in the love triangle. The following stanza, in turn, opens the account of his "ire" and "grete myght" in battle; it initiates the final (though interrupted) portion of the narrative leading up to the hero's death.

The epilogue does not (it would seem) constitute a clearly defined or strictly differentiated section of the poem, and there is room for doubt as to whether Chaucer actually regarded the conclusion of his poem as a formal epilogue. In contrast to the *prohemia* or prologues of the first four books, the epilogue is not designated by either an *incipit* or an *explicit*. There is an *envoi* embedded in the narrative, to be sure; but, unlike the majority of Chaucer's *envois*, it is not labeled as such, nor does it occur at the very end of the poem.

In contrast with Chaucer's prologues in the *Troilus* and his *envois* in other works,[7] his epilogue does not appear to be a clearly defined section of the poem. Except for the five last stanzas of

---

[7] Chaucer or his scribes usually distinguish "prologues" or "proems" from the narrative proper. The *Canterbury Tales* designates the "prologe" of the Reeve's tale and those of the Cook, the Wife of Bath, the Friar, the Summoner, the Clerk, the Merchant, the Franklin, the Pardoner, the Prioress, the Nun's Priest, the Second Nun, the Canon's Yeoman, the Manciple, and the Parson. The *House of Fame* distinguishes the various subsections of the poem: "Proem," "Invocation," and "Story" in Book I; "Proem" and "Dream" in Book II; "Invocation" and "Dream" in Book III. In *Anelida and Arcita*, "Invocation," "Story," Anelida's "Complaint," and the continuation of the story are clearly marked. The *prohemium* to the *Legend of Good Women* is identified by an *explicit*. The *Complaint of Mars* contains separate designations for "Proem," "Story," "Compleynt," etc.

Chaucer's prologues are usually more complex and more extensive than his concluding passages, and separate designations for the latter are less frequent. The final section of the *Canterbury Tales* has received several alternative headings: "Heere taketh the makere of this book his leve," "*Hic capit Autor licenciam*," "*Preces de Chauceres*," etc. The Clerk's Tale concludes with stanzas addressed to "noble wyves" and "archewyves" and labeled "Lenvoy de Chaucer"; and the heading "Lenvoy" occurs before the final verses of several shorter poems: *Fortune, Lak of Stedfastnesse, The Complaint of Venus*, the *Lenvoys* to Scogan and Bukton, and *The Complaint of Chaucer to his Purse*. In *Anelida and Arcita*, the "Conclusion" of Anelida's complaint receives a separate designation.

application, exhortation, and prayer, he seems to have been reluctant to make a formal division between his narrative conclusion and his valedictory appeals; the latter are interwoven with the end of the story.

In the absence of a clear-cut beginning for the epilogue and scribal notations designating it as a separate section, we should be cautious in applying this term to the end of Chaucer's romance. Since it is too firmly established in contemporary criticism to be discarded, we should place it in imaginary brackets.

4

Like its apparent prolixity, the inconsistency of the epilogue seems to have been greatly exaggerated; variety and diversity have been mistaken for contradiction. Not only have the various sections of Chaucer's conclusion been linked together by common themes but they also share the same Boethian frame of reference in common with the rest of the poem. Against a fourteenth-century background, the Christian elements in the final stanzas are less irrelevant than they have seemed to several modern readers. Though the author has given his romance a pagan setting, though he has usually observed decorum in depicting "payens corsed olde rites" and "alle hire goddes," he remains essentially a medieval Catholic writing for Catholic readers. It is scarcely surprising, therefore, that he should allude to Christian commonplaces in passages of direct address to a Christian audience. Nor would his transition from Boethian to Christian *topoi* seem improbable to his contemporaries. Some of them shared Dante's respect for Boethius as a Christian theologian and martyr. Moreover, on such doctrinal points as the *visio dei* and divine foreknowledge, the teachings of the *Consolation* closely approximated those of the Church; Pseudo-Aquinas interpreted this treatise from an orthodox point of view.

Nor are Troilus's flight to the heavens and his contempt of the world incompatible with the rest of the poem. These motifs are just as relevant to the *Troilus* as to the *Pharsalia* and the *Teseida*. Though the flight sequence is a later insertion, it does not constitute a second ending, nor is it incompatible with the passages that precede and follow it. In the context of the revised epilogue it is essentially an amplification of the earlier version of Troilus's death. By definition, this consisted in the separation of body and soul. In portraying the separate ends of flesh and spirit, Chaucer has not given his poem a "double ending";[8] he has simply amplified the original catastrophe, complementing his terse and (from a theological viewpoint) incomplete report of Troilus's end with an account of the fate of his soul. The hero's own insights dramatically underscore the separation of soul and body.

Far from violating the unity of the *Troilus*, the flight stanzas increase its coherence, providing an effective transition from the story itself to the moral generalizations of the concluding stanzas. As a final addition to the narrative, they complete the poet's image of false happiness by including the hero's achievement of true felicity. As the concluding phase of a narrative *exemplum*, they give particular and concrete expression to concepts that had already received abstract statement in the last stanzas of the original epilogue. They provide inductive support for the arguments of Chaucer's exhortations to the "yonge . . . folkes" and to Gower and Strode.

In the revised epilogue, the dominant theme of the concluding stanzas—the antithesis between worldly vanity and true felicity —is announced and developed in the flight sequence. The moral vision of the author's commentary has become an integral part of the story, the climax and conclusion of the narrative. The poet's insights are extended to the hero of the poem. Chaucer has, in a sense, partly surrendered to Troilus himself the privilege of judging the central action of the poem and of delivering the verdict on the meaning and value of his romance. Concluding the narrative action with an act of contemplation, he embodies the *moralitas* of the poem in the hero's own recognition of the truth. Focusing his scattered reflections on worldly felicity into a single insight, the poet concentrates the multiple ironies of action and

---

[8] Cf. Theodore A. Stroud, "Boethius' Influence on Chaucer's *Troilus*," *MP*, XLIX (1951-1952), 1-9, on the "double ending" of the poem, or "the duality of the epilogue."

situation, character and thought, into a final burst of ghostly laughter.

5

In retracting "the book of Troilus" at the end of the *Canterbury Tales*, Chaucer condemned "worldly vanitees" in language remarkably similar to that of the *Troilus* epilogue. In the flight sequence Troilus himself had despised "This wrecched world, and held al vanite To respect of the pleyn felicite That is in hevene above . . ." The poet himself had joined his hero in contempt of the world, exhorting the "yonge . . . folkes" to repair "hom fro worldly vanyte" and inveighing against "thise wrecched worldes appetites." In taking "his leve," the "makere" of the *Tales* included his tragedy among the "translacions and enditynges of worldly vanitees, the whiche I revoke in my retracciouns. . . ."[9]

As the same *topos* occurs in both conclusions, one might reasonably infer that both are retractations. Since Chaucer retracts the *Troilus* in the *Tales* on the grounds of "worldly vanitees," is not the epilogue to his romance likewise a retractation? Perhaps it may be, but only in a very limited sense. The *Troilus* epilogue is not a formal *retractatio*, like the "retracciouns" in the *Canterbury Tales*. Nor does it possess the juridical formalities—accusation and defense, submission and penance—of the mock-serious arraignment for "heresye ageyns my lawe" in *The Legend of Good Women*. To exhort from worldly vanity at the conclusion of a romance that has portrayed "worldly vanitees" does not constitute a formal "retraccioun" of the romance itself. Whether in game or in earnest, in literature or in law, a *retractatio* is a formal act involving explicit recantation of particular works or doctrines. There is no explicit retractation in the epilogue of the *Troilus*.

Moreover, the negative attitudes expressed in the epilogue towards "worldly vanyte" are inherent in the poem itself. They are implicit in the Boethian framework of Chaucer's romance and

<hr>

[9] F. N. Robinson, *The Works of Geoffrey Chaucer*, 2d ed. (Boston, 1957), p. 265.

in his conception of the *Troilus* as a tragic *exemplum*. The *contemptus mundi* expressed in the *fyn* stanza is directed not only toward earthly love and "lust," but toward the entire complex of worldly goods and earthly felicity. Since Chaucer has repeatedly stressed their mutability, he has little to recant. Instead, he faces a task comparable to that of Dame Philosophy in the *Consolation*; having demonstrated the nature of false felicity and false goods, he must now direct his readers to the supreme Good and point out the nature of true happiness. His epilogue completes the Boethian framework of his poem, complementing the Boethian commonplaces he had already exploited in portraying the instability of earthly happiness, with an exhortation to a true and "sothfast" beatitude. The fact that Chaucer urges his readers to seek an eternal Good outside and beyond the limits of his poem, that he is aware of the mutability of language and the transiency of literature, strengthens the emphasis on worldly vanity and *contemptus mundi* in the epilogue, but it does not constitute a formal retractation of the poem itself. If tragedy is really a *carmen reprehensivum*, recantation may seem superfluous; like the Monk's tragedies of Adam and Samson, the tragedy of Troilus did not actually need retractation.

Finally, the negative attitudes expressed in the epilogue toward Troilus's affair with Criseyde are consistent with traditional conceptions of his end as a tragic example, a mirror in which other lovers might behold the fatal consequences of loving unwisely. In *The Parliament of Fowls* Troilus is depicted on the walls of Venus's temple among illustrious lovers and tragic victims of love—Pyramus, Tristram, Cleopatra, Semiramis, and others:[10]

> Alle these were peynted on that other syde,
> And al here love, and in what plyt they dyde.

In the *Filostrato* Troilo's example is proposed as a warning to young men to love wisely. Like Othello, he has loved not wisely but too well, and his premature death through a "wicked lady" (*ria donna*) should encourage other lovers to exercise greater

---

[10] *Ibid.*, p. 313.

discretion in selecting a mistress. In the *Troilus* also the hero's fatal love affair serves as a tragic *exemplum*; indeed, the poet formally designates his work as a *tragedye*. Finally, in *The Legend of Good Women*, Chaucer would defend the *Troilus* as an "ensample" to beware of falseness and vice.[11]

According to the tradition Chaucer had inherited, Troilus must inevitably be betrayed by his mistress and perish miserably in battle. He must inevitably be a victim of Venus and a martyr of love. His fate must serve as a warning to other lovers—an example to be shunned rather than imitated—and one might reasonably expect the poet to address some sort of *suasoria* to the youth (*giovanetti* or "yonge fresshe folkes") exhorting them to love more wisely. This is precisely what we find in the *Troilus*. Though Chaucer has altered the *topoi* he found in Boccaccio's exhortation and introduced Boethian commonplaces into the *fyn* stanza, the critical attitude he displays toward Troilus's love affair is traditional.

If there is an element of "repudiation" in the epilogue (though one would prefer the term "criticism"), it is not inconsistent with the poem as a whole. On the contrary, it is inherent in the poet's basic conception of his *tragedye* and in his immediate source. Like the tragedy of Samson and Delilah, the tragedy of Troilus and Criseyde was a story of misplaced trust. Ending tragically, it served as a negative *exemplum*, and the reader should not be dismayed to encounter a negative stance in Chaucer's epilogue, as in Boccaccio's.

---

[11] In the prologue to the *Legend of Good Women* the story of Troilus and Criseyde is represented as a negative or admonitory example (text G, lines 456-464; Robinson, *Geoffrey Chaucer*, pp. 493-494):

> Ne a trewe lovere oghte me nat to blame,
> Thogh that I speke a fals lovere som shame.
> They oughte rathere with me for to holde,
> For that I of Criseyde wrot or tolde,
> Or of the Rose; what so myn auctour mente,
> Algate, God wot, it was myn entente
> To forthere trouthe in love and it cheryce,
> And to be war fro falsnesse and fro vice
> By swich ensaumple; this was my menynge.

6

Since the *Troilus* is widely regarded as an encomium of courtly love,[12] critics have, not unreasonably, interpreted the epilogue in this light. Some have been puzzled by Chaucer's apparent repudiation of the ideals of courtly love. Some have raised the question of his sincerity. Did he really mean what he wrote in his final stanzas, or was he merely paying a conventional obeisance to clerical orthodoxy? Or did he perhaps, like Ovid's Medea, "see and approve the better" but follow, or at least feel a stronger sympathy for, the worse? For one reader, however, the flight sequence represented the apotheosis of the courtly lover; in his opinion, Chaucer's revision had altered not only the context but the meaning of the *fyn* stanza.[13] Instead of referring to Troilus's miserable death, it now pointed directly to the celestial reward he had merited through obedience to the principles of *amour courtois*. Others have cast doubt on the meaning and historical

[12] Cf. William George Dodd, *Courtly Love in Chaucer and Gower*, *Harvard Studies in English*, vol. I (Boston, 1913); Eugene Edward Slaughter, *Virtue According to Love—in Chaucer* (New York, 1957); Thomas A. Kirby, *Chaucer's Troilus: A Study in Courtly Love*, *Louisiana State University Studies*, no. XXXIX (University, 1940); Alexander J. Denomy, C.S.B., *The Heresy of Courtly Love* (New York, 1947); Denomy, "The Two Moralities of Chaucer's *Troilus and Criseyde*," *Transactions of the Royal Society of Canada*, vol. XLIV, series III, sec. 2 (June, 1950), pp. 35-46; C. S. Lewis, *The Allegory of Love, A Study in Medieval Tradition* (Oxford, 1936). Denomy ("Two Moralities") regards Chaucer's epilogue as a "retraction" or "Palinode"; Chaucer "repudiates Courtly Love . . . not only in the Palinode but within the fabric of the story itself."

[13] Cf. Kirby, *Chaucer's Troilus*, p. 282, "Stanza 262 . . . is particularly significant in that it reiterates for the last time Chaucer's conception of Troilus as the ideal lover. On his death the hero ascends directly to heaven; he lingers in no limbo, no purgatory; there is no period of purgation of any kind. On the contrary, his love has been so noble, so spiritual, that he passes at once to his eternal reward." Cf. Peter Dronke, "The Conclusion of Troilus and Criseyde," *Medium AEvum*, XXXIII (1964), 47-52, "Troilus' love and death and heavenly reward form a unity. He does not . . . win his salvation *per accidens* . . . he wins it 'for love'; he wins a place, not in the sphere of the Moon . . . but in the eighth sphere, the highest heaven open to human beings."

validity of "courtly love,"[14] arguing that the stereotype of *amour courtois* as a "system" is largely the creation of late nineteenth- and early twentieth-century scholarship.

We are scarcely in a position to judge whether or not Chaucer has repudiated courtly love in his epilogue, until we achieve a clearer idea of what the term actually means and of how far it is truly relevant for the *Troilus*. The term itself is not altogether anachronistic. It appears occasionally in medieval Continental literature and in Elizabethan poetry. Indeed it provides the nominal argument of Sir John Davies's *Orchestra or, A Poem on Dancing*:[15]

> The courtly love Antinous did make—
> Antinous, that fresh and jolly knight
> Which of the gallants that did undertake
> To win the widow had most wealth and might,
> Wit to persuade, and beauty to delight—
> The courtly love he made unto the queen
> Homer forgot, as if it had not been.

Later in the poem Davies applies the same term to the sea:[16]

> And to make known his courtly love the more
> He oft doth lay aside his three-fork'd mace
> And with his arms the timorous earth embrace.

The scene of Antinous's exhortations is a royal court, crowded with suitors for Penelope's hand. His "courtly love" is associated

---

[14] For recent criticism of the concept of courtly love, see D. W. Robertson, Jr., "Chaucerian Tragedy," *ELH*, XIX (1952), 1-37; Robertson, *A Preface to Chaucer*, pp. 391-503; John F. Benton, "The Court of Champagne as a Literary Center," *Speculum*, XXXVI (1961), 551-591. *The Meaning of Courtly Love*, ed. F. X. Newman (Albany, 1968) contains essays by Robertson, Benton, Charles S. Singleton, W. T. H. Jackson, and Theodore Silverstein, and a selected bibliography on the theory of courtly love. See also James Lyndon Shanley, "The *Troilus* and Christian Love," *ELH*, VI (1939), 271-281.

[15] Gerald Bullett, ed., *Silver Poets of the Sixteenth Century* (London and New York, 1964), p. 320. Professor E. Talbot Donaldson has already noted this passage. I am indebted to Professor Elizabeth Story Donno for valuable criticism of this chapter and for a reference to Professor Donaldson's *Speaking of Chaucer* (London, 1970).

[16] *Ibid.*, p. 328.

with the manners of a courtier and the virtues of a knight. The poet emphasizes his "noblesse" and "splendour of mind," his "fair manners," and (above all) his clever and courtly rhetoric:[17]

> Sing then, Terpsichore, my light Muse, sing
> His gentle art and cunning courtesy!

Though Davies's poem belongs to the late Renaissance and can therefore throw only limited light on medieval conventions, it is nevertheless significant as an example of the continuity and transformation of medieval tradition in a Renaissance context. The *Orchestra* is court poetry, and the author has adapted his *topoi* to the tastes of Elizabeth's court and the court of James I. Antinous's "courtly love" is essentially an invitation to a courtly dance, and Davies concludes his poem with a tribute to a queen who delighted in dancing—a taste that provoked the sarcastic wit of an ambassador.

The *Orchestra* inevitably bears the marks of its Renaissance origin, but it also exhibits several points of similarity or dissimilarity with modern conceptions of courtly love. It too portrays a courtly setting, persons of knightly or royal rank, chivalric virtues and courtly manners, and the erotic ceremonial of formal courtship. Nevertheless, Antinous's wooing is neither secret nor (on the surface) illicit; he believes (or hopes) Ulysses to be dead, and he is openly seeking Penelope as a wife, not as a secret paramour. With its emphasis on "courtly dancings" and on decorum ("Now keeping state, now humbly honouring low, And ever for the persons and the place He taught most fit and best according grace") the *Orchestra* would appear to provide some foundation for the conception of "courtly love" as a feature of literary decorum. It contains no suggestion, however, of *amour courtois* as a "system." In this respect it is in accord with the views of several contemporary scholars.

In the light of recent criticism, it would be prudent to suspend judgment as to the historical or literary validity of courtly love. Several of its principal features are, in fact, explicable in terms of

---

[17] *Ibid.*, p. 321.

conventional poetic or rhetorical theory;[18] and one does not have
to resort to the hypothesis of a historical "system" in order to
account for them. For our immediate purposes it is enough that
Troilus observes the decorum of a lover of noble birth and
character in a sophisticated and courtly society. In his clandestine
love affair with a gentlewoman of lower rank, Troilus acts,
speaks, and feels in a manner befitting his age, his birth, and his
station. Throughout the poem, he exhibits the *gentilesse* and
curteisye appropriate to a knight and a prince of the blood royal.
In short, he brings to his romance with Criseyde the same
nobility and courtesy of mind and manners that he would be
expected to display in other pursuits. In this sense he embodies
the "idea" of a "courtly" or "gentle" (i.e., noble) lover, and in this
limited sense the *Troilus* can be regarded as an "idealization" of
"courtly love."

In the pursuit of love, as in other vocations and avocations,
there can be good and bad manners, aristocratic and vulgar
conventions, "U" and "non-U" behavior. Like the arts of rhetoric
and poetic, the art of love can display a high style and a low
style—and perhaps a middle style. The contrary of *curteisye* is
vileinye, and this may be as significant for the decorum of the
lover as for the manners of different classes of society. Boccaccio
himself stressed this antithesis, paradoxically condemning haughty
noblewomen as base or *vili*—beasts rather than true gentlewomen!—and branding Criseida herself as *villana*. Chaucer, however, suppressed both of these passages. Instead of the antithesis
between courtly[19] and churlish love, he emphasizes the opposition

---

[18] Cf. John Steadman, "'Courtly Love' as a Problem of Style," in *Chaucer
und seine Zeit: Symposion für Walter F. Schirmer*, ed. Arno Esch (Tübingen,
1968), pp. 1-33.

[19] Courtly love is sometimes contrasted with divine love as though they
were logical contraries. If we are to use these terms at all—to control them
instead of being controlled by them—it would be advisable to define them (and
their opposites) more exactly. If the opposite of *curteisye* is *vileinye*, then the
opposite of courtly love would appear to be churlish or base love. The
opposite of divine love would be earthly love. Rational love would be opposed
to irrational lust, spiritual to carnal affection, and sacred to profane, etc. These

between earthly and heavenly devotion, between love of the creature and love of the Creator. Instead of stressing the contrast between "courtesy" and "villainy" in love, he contrasted the service of a mistress or the service of Venus and Amor with the service of the true God. He did not literally condemn "courtly love" either in his own person or in that of Troilus. (Indeed, he did not use the term at all.) His condemnation was less specific and far more comprehensive; he condemned "blynde lust" (concupiscence and pleasure) and "wrecched worldes appetites." To *Frauendienst* he opposed *Gottesdienst*.

7

"Aut prodesse volunt aut delectare poetae." Like many of his contemporaries, Chaucer shared Horace's opinion that the poet should aim at profit or delight, mixing *utile* with *dulce* and combining "sentence" with "solaas." A commonplace of classical theory, the conception of poetry as a sort of sugared pill— wholesome but bitter instruction made palatable by sweetness of discourse—passed into medieval rhetoric and poetic, and ultimately into Renaissance criticism.

In Boethius's *Consolation*, Chaucer encountered a similar conception of poetry and rhetoric as instruments of moral persuasion, a conception that closely resembled the Horatian ideal. Dame Philosophy herself had possessed the apothecary's art of tempering a bitter medicine with palatable words, and "the swetnesse of here dite" had left her disciple "astoned" and "desyrous

---

categories may, of course, overlap; Troilus's affection could be described as simultaneously earthly and courtly, irrational and carnal. We should also note the ambiguity of the term "courtly love" or "Court Amours" in Renaissance usage. In Davies's poem the former term is used not only in a court setting but also (more specifically) in the context of courtship or wooing. In Milton's allusion to "Court Amours" the primary emphasis falls apparently on the courtly milieu. It is interesting to note, however, that just as Davies introduces the *topos* of courtly love in connection with the dance, Milton introduces it in association with allusions to "Mixt Dance, or wanton Mask, or Midnight Bal / Or Serenate, which the starv'd Lover sings / To his proud fair, best quitted with disdain."

of herknynge" further.[20] Conveying her teachings through poetry as well as prose, through rhetorical exhortations as well as by logical demonstrations, she had administered "lyghtere medicynes" at first, in order to prepare her patient for stronger remedies later: "so that thilke passiouns that ben waxen hard in swellynge by perturbacions flowynge into thy thought, mowen waxen esy and softe to resceyven the strengthe of a more myghty and more egre medicyne, by an esyere touchynge."[21]

In thus mixing sweet and sour, doctrinal instruction and pleasant persuasion, Dame Philosophy came close to usurping the office of the poet. Boethius's dialogue not only alternates verse with prose but as a dramatic fiction it approaches the frontiers of poetry. These analogies between the roles of the poet and philosopher made it easier for Chaucer to graft the commonplaces of Boethian ethics into his own poetic *tragedye*, not as dead or leafless branches, but as living tissue capable of bearing fruit. If Dame Philosophy could assume the responsibilities of the poet, Chaucer in turn might undertake those of the moral philosopher.

In the tradition of the *consolatio*, moral philosophy generally serves as the principal remedy against Fortune's changes and the turbulence of human passions. In Seneca's epistles and dialogues, it administers consolation in adversity and advises restraint in prosperity. In Petrarch's treatise, it is a "remedy" against prosperity and adversity alike. In Boethius's dialogue, it is a "medicyne" that may dispel grief or fear in regard to worldly adversity, and excessive joy or hope in worldly prosperity. This would appear to be one of the functions of Boethian philosophy in the *Troilus*. By introducing into his secular love story, with its abrupt changes of Fortune without and passion within, the commonplaces of Boethian ethics—the mutability of Fortune's goods, the "stable feyth" and providence controlling the vicissitudes of time, and the distinction between true and false felicity—Chaucer has mixed *utile* with *dulce* and profit with delight. Like Dame

---

[20] Boethius, Book III, prose 1.
[21] *Ibid.*, Book I, prose 5.

Philosophy, he has sweetened his "egre medicyne." Or perhaps, conversely, he has merely added medicine to his sweetmeats.

Whether the *utile* or the *dulce* was foremost in the author's mind is an open question, and no attempt will be made to resolve it here. The fact that most of us today, and perhaps many of the poet's contemporaries, have valued the *Troilus* chiefly for its "solaas" rather than for its "sentence" proves nothing about the author's intent. Clearly he had both ends in mind, and he apparently succeeded in striking a balance between them. He did not (it would seem) sacrifice one to the other; nor should we.

In the epilogue Chaucer took deliberate pains to "moralize" his story, drawing the appropriate inferences and ethical *sententiae* from the narrative, emphasizing final causes, and exhorting his readers to seek their proper end or true happiness. In thus centering the conclusion of his story and his exhortation to his audience on the idea of felicity, he consciously aligned his epilogue with the traditional orientation of ethical doctrine, the end and felicity of man. In this respect, like Dante's allegory and Boethius's fictive dialogue, the epilogue of the *Troilus* served the end of moral philosophy.

Nevertheless, the epilogue is only a part, albeit an important one, of the poem as a whole. It exists for the poem, not the poem for the epilogue. In investigating its intellectual background and its thematic relationships with the rest of the *Troilus*, the critic runs the risk of leaving an unbalanced impression of the poet's intent, emphasizing profit at the expense of pleasure and subordinating *delectare* to *prodesse*. Because this section consciously points a moral, a study devoted to the epilogue may seem to overstress the ethical element in the narrative as a whole. The poet's explicit *moralitas*—the ethical inferences he desired his readers to draw from the narrative—does not and cannot comprehend the total complex of meanings implicit in the story. These cannot be reduced to a single formula or *sententia*, even if the formula is Chaucer's own.

Chaucer obviously wrote his romance in order to delight as well as instruct; and perhaps in his intention *delectare* was a more immediate and a more attractive end than *prodesse*. Perhaps, indeed, the delight he sought to arouse through his narrative was not the sort of pleasure that a moral philosopher, or even the poet himself as moralist, could altogether approve.

Though there is a tension between the traditional ends of poetry—instruction and delight—these functions are not mutually exclusive, and they need not lead to inconsistency. Chaucer managed to reconcile both of these ends through the irony implicit in his Boethian point of view. (Even though "Chaucerian irony" has become a facile cliché that lends itself all too readily to critical abuse, it is nevertheless of cardinal significance for Chaucer's literary exploitation of Boethian commonplaces.) The contrast between the philosopher's knowledge of true happiness and the blindness of ambitious or voluptuous worldlings ignorant of their true Good dominated the *Consolation of Philosophy*, and it had similarly left its mark on the apotheosis tradition. Complementing the irony of Lucan and Boethius, the irony of the *Troilus* enables the poet to "delight" his readers through the details of a secular love story, in full awareness that such delight is transitory and that the story itself belongs in the catalogue of "worldly vanitees."

8

The intellectual and literary tradition behind Chaucer's flight passage is notably varied and complex, including Neoplatonic and Stoic pneumatology and medieval astronomy, scholastic theology and Boethian ethics. The motifs of the flight of the mind to the heavens, and the soul's ascent to the stars are widely diffused and exhibit a proportionally wide range of variants. Not infrequently they are associated specifically with the contemplation of heaven and earth and the comparison between worldly and celestial goods. We have encountered instances of this combination in the apotheoses of Pompey and Arcita, in the visionary ascents of Dante and Scipio, and in the speculative flights that Boethius's Philosophy promises her disciples. The *contemptus mundi* theme is prominent in most of these analogues, and in three of them —the *Pharsalia*, the *Commedia*, and the *Teseida*—the hero's disdain finds overt expression in laughter. As to the destination of these voyagers there is significant diversity. The *manes* of Pompey and Arcita apparently reach the lunar concave—the traditional site of Elysium "according to the theologians." Dante and Scipio attain the sphere of the fixed stars. Dame Philosophy promises her followers an abode beyond the spheres, and Dante himself passes subsequently to the Empyrean. In Lucan and Boccaccio, as in Chaucer, the flight passage occurs in a heroic context—in "epic" or "tragic" poetry.

In most of these analogues, the celestial flight is associated with cognition, with knowledge of the truth or vision of the highest Good. Like Chaucer, the Stoic and Neoplatonic philosophers emphasize the contemplative felicity of the separated soul; the Stoics especially dwell on the delights the natural philosopher may find in contemplating the movements of the heavens. Boethius stresses the knowledge and recovery of true felicity. One medieval commentator on Lucan interprets Pompey's ascent as a return to rational motions, and others emphasize the contrast between earthly ignorance and celestial knowledge. Boccaccio similarly stresses the ignorance of humanity, but applies this commonplace primarily to the antithesis between true and false beauty. For most of these writers, as for Chaucer, the ascent represents a return to true knowledge—to pure cognition undarkened by the passions and appetites of the body—and to the soul's native region or *patria*.

In the epilogue Chaucer's emphasis falls primarily on the antithesis between mutability and constancy, between changing and unchanging goods, or transitory and stable felicity. Standing on the frontier between sublunary change and celestial steadfastness, attended by the winged god of reason, Troilus can perceive at last the distinction between constant and inconstant goods, between true and false beatitude.

Chaucer has modified these stanzas from the *Teseida* just as he had altered the epilogue (and much of the narrative) of the *Filostrato*. In both cases he has increased the Boethian elements he found in Boccaccio's poems, accentuating the *contemptus mundi* theme. Since this motif was common to the flight passages of Lucan and Dante and to Christian and classical ethics, it is not surprising that Chaucer (who had already translated Boethius's *Consolation* and Pope Innocent's *De contemptu mundi*) should emphasize this theme in his epilogue.

The *contemptus mundi* theme is notably absent, however, from the epilogue of the *Filostrato*. Boccaccio alludes to the vainglory of young women and to Troilo's "speranza vana" in Criseida, but he does not condemn worldly vanities. We look in vain for the *topoi* we find in Chaucer's corresponding stanzas: "false worldes brotelnesse," "worldly vanyte," "wrecched worldes appetites!" The *Teseida*, however, places greater stress on this motif. Arcita regards the earth as "da nulla stimare a rispetto del ciel," and he condemns "la vanitate . . . dell'umane genti," who pursue the false beauty of the world. In the *Troilus*, the hero's contempt for worldly vanity is expressed in even stronger terms. He despises "This *wrecched* world" and holds "*al* vanite To respect of the pleyn felicite That is in hevene above," damning "*al* oure werk that folweth so The blynde lust, the which that may nat laste. . . ." (Italics mine.) The totality of earthly values—*terrena*, *temporalia*, *mundana*—falls under Troilus's sweeping condemnation.

In this last passage Chaucer may have introduced a Christian allusion. "Lust" may signify both pleasure and concupiscence. In the former sense it recalls Boethius's condemnation of the transitory nature of worldly pleasure (*voluptas*), but in the latter sense it is reminiscent of Saint John's dehortation against love of the world (I John 2.17): "And the world passeth away, and the lust thereof. . . ." ("Et mundus transit, & concupiscentia eius. Qui autem facit voluntatem Dei manet in aeternum.")

In the flight passage, with its pagan hero, Chaucer prudently observes verisimilitude. This Scriptural allusion (if such it is) does not seem obtrusive, nor does it violate the decorum of "payens corsed olde rites." In his valedictory appeals, however, the poet has greater license to amplify it, and he returns to the Boethian, and Biblical, motif of the world's transiency:

> . . . and thynketh al nys but a faire
> This world, that passeth soone as floures faire.

In contrasting divine fidelity with the world's fickleness, and divine stability with earthly vicissitudes:

> For he nyl falsen no wight, dar I seye,
> That wol his herte al holly on hym leye

Chaucer exploited a commonplace that belonged to Boethian and biblical traditions alike. Both had stressed the transitory nature of the world and its goods in contrast with the Creator's eternity. Both had exhorted the reader to place his faith in divine rather than in earthly goods. Biblical persuasions to *fiducia* and *spes* in divine providence paralleled Boethius's assurance that it was neither "in ydel ne in veyn" that men "put in God hope and preyeris. . . ." In both traditions, moreover, the opposition between divine steadfastness and secular change had found expression in astronomical terms. Boethius had cited the heavens as an instance of the "stable feyth" whereby "the world . . . varieth accordable chaungynges" under the government of divine providence. The Epistle of James had (1:17) similarly contrasted the stability of the "Father of lights" with the change and vicissitudes of the world: "Omne datum optimum, & omne datum perfectum desursum est, descendens a Patre luminum, apud quem non est transmutatio, nec vicissitudinis obumbratio."

Having mounted to the region of the stars, beyond the realm of sublunary change, Troilus (like Lucan's Pompey, Boccaccio's Arcita, Shelley's Adonais, and other apotheosized heroes) has "outsoared the shadow of our night." He has reached "a perdurable seete" above variableness and shadow of turning—a steadfast good common to both classical and Christian tradition.

INDEX